MORE
SCIENCE
ACTIVITIES

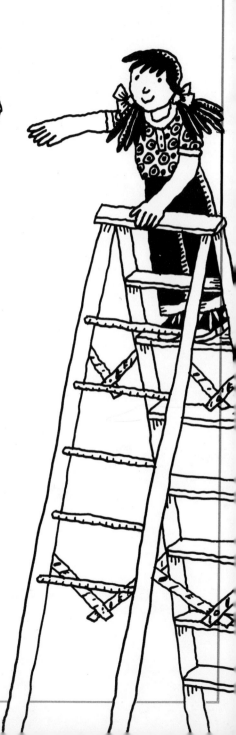

FROM THE SMITHSONIAN INSTITUTION

MORE SCIENCE ACTIVITIES

GALISON BOOKS
GMG PUBLISHING, NEW YORK
AND
SCIENCE LEARNING, INC.
ANNAPOLIS, MARYLAND

A Galison Book
Published by GMG Publishing Corp.
25 W. 43rd Street
New York, NY 10036

ISBN 0-939456-16-8

Project Director: John Falk, Ph.D.
Authors: Megan Stine, Craig Gillespie, Gladys Stanbury,
Laurie Greenberg, Jamie Harms, Sharon Maves,
Larry Malone, Carol Moroz-Henry
Reviewer: Kathy Faggella

Designer: Marilyn Rose
Design Assistant: Christine Kirk
Illustrator: Simms Taback
Editor: Cheryl Solimini
Production Editor: Nora Galvin
Publisher: Gerald Galison

Fourth Printing

CONTENTS

INTRODUCTION

Science and technology touches nearly every facet of our lives today. By the 21st century, our society will demand that all its citizens possess basic competencies in the fundamentals of science and the use of technology. As science increasingly becomes the dominant subject of the work place, it is important to begin developing within children an understanding and appreciation of science early in their lives.

Learning can, and does, occur in many places and many situations. Learning occurs in school, at home, and on the trip between home and school. This book provides suggestions for interactive science activities that can be done in a variety of settings, using inexpensive and readily available materials. Whether the activities are done in a classroom or in a home, they will provide adults and children with increased opportunities to explore natural phenomenon in an engaging and exciting way. Included are experiments, activities, crafts, and games that allow you, whether teacher or parent, to learn science along with your children. The only requirements for success are the directions provided with each activity, a few common household items, a little bit of time, and some curiosity and imagination. The activities in this book are designed as curricular materials, educational guides for you to use in teaching science.

SOME SUGGESTIONS FOR TEACHERS

The activities in this book should be used as supplements to your normal classroom science curricula. Since they were originally developed for use in out-of-school situations, they may require some minor modifications to permit a larger number of children to participate. Nonetheless, you will find that these activities lend themselves well to a fun-filled science lesson for all participants.

An increasing number of school districts are exploring the use of "take-home" lessons in order to build stronger learning partnership bonds between parents and teachers, home and school. These materials have proven to be an excellent source for such "team-building" efforts. Both teachers and parents find these activities rewarding ways to provide quality learning experiences for children.

SOME SUGGESTIONS FOR PARENTS

One of the most important jobs that you have, as a parent, is the education of your children. Every day is filled with opportunities for you to *actively* participate in your child's learning. Together you can explore the natural world and make connections between classroom lessons and real-life situations. You will learn the value of asking good questions, as well as strategies for finding answers to those questions.

FOR BOTH TEACHERS AND PARENTS

The best things you can bring to each activity are your experience, your interest, and, most importantly, your enthusiasm. These materials were designed to be both educational and enjoyable. They offer opportunities for discovery, creative thinking, and fun.

HOW TO USE THIS BOOK

The science activities in this book can be successfully implemented by any interested adult, regardless of his or her science background. Accordingly, the above have been designed so there is no one "correct" solution and no "right" way to do it. Do not be afraid to say "I don't know!"

There are twenty activities in this book; since every classroom and family is different, not all activities will be equally suitable. Take the time to browse through the book and find the ones that seem to make sense for your class or family. There is no prescribed order to these activities, nor any necessity to do all of them. Once you have selected an activity to do, take the time to read through it before you attempt to do it.

At the beginning of each activity is a list of all the materials you will need to do the project. Try to assemble all of these items before you begin. The procedures have been laid out in an easy-to-follow, step-by-step guide. If you follow these directions, you should have no difficulty doing the activity. Once you have completed the basic activity, there are also suggested variations that you can try, now or later. At the end of each activity is an "Afterwords" section. This section is for you, the adult. It is intended to provide additional information, not on how to help children but for the interest of an adult participant—take some time to read it for your own enjoyment.

ASKING QUESTIONS

Encourage your children to ask questions, even if you don't know the answers. The essence of science is asking questions, and then trying to find out the answers. Some of the answers can be discovered in books, some through observation, and some, at present, are unanswerable by anyone. Ask questions like:

(before you start)
"What do you think is going to happen when we do this experiment?"
(during the activity)
"What do you see?"
"Does this remind you of anything else you've ever seen?"
(after the activity is completed)
"What do you know about X now, that you didn't know before we started?"

"Is there anything you don't understand? How can we find out the answer?"

Encourage all kinds of answers, and all kinds of questions. Sometimes the crazy ones are the ones that work. Often there is more than one answer to a question, so be tolerant of diversity and open to multiple solutions. Use the library or an encyclopedia to help answer questions and further your understanding. Lead, or have a child lead, a discussion after the project is completed. This will help to pull together what happened, why things happened, and what the activity was all about. Just remember that it may take more than one exposure for some of the ideas introduced in these activities to "sink in." These activities are beginnings, not endings. Finally, don't be afraid to be a learner yourself—that was a large part of why these activities were developed in the first place. They are for learning, adults and children *together*.

John H. Falk, Ph.D.
President
Science Learning, Inc.

GINGER ALE

GINGER ALE

Ginger ale takes about an hour and one-half to prepare. It must be bottled after six hours. Ginger ale will taste best if you wait two days before drinking.

YOU WILL NEED

Pot filled with 4 quarts water
3 Tablespoons ginger
½ Lime
2½ Cups sugar
3 Tablespoons cream of tartar
1 Tablespoon baker's yeast
Cheesecloth or coffee filter
Funnel, mixing spoon, stove
Gallon jug with cap or cork

Have you ever wondered what makes ginger ale fizzy? All the little bubbles you see when you open a bottle of ginger ale are carbon dioxide —a gas that's in the air you breathe. Because bubbly drinks have carbon dioxide, they are often called *carbonated* drinks.

But how does the carbon dioxide get into the drink? The key is something called yeast. Yeast makes the differ-ence between "flat" water and fizzy soda. See the differ-ence for yourself when you mix water, yeast and flavorings to make your own ginger ale.

WHAT IS YEAST?

Yeasts are tiny, living plants. They are not active in your refrigerator because the cold keeps them in hibernation. But when you put them in a warm, moist place and give them sugar to eat, they get ac-tive and make carbon dioxide gas. This gas can make bread rise or drinks fizzy.

You can put a little yeast into a closed jug with warm, sugary water. As long as the yeast have enough sugar to eat, they'll keep making car-bon dioxide. When the air space above the water fills with carbon dioxide, the gas bubbles can't escape and they stay in the water. This makes the water carbonated. If the cap is loose, all the car-bon dioxide will escape from the jug. You'll get "flat" ginger ale.

1 Boil the water in the pot. Add:
■ Three tablespoons ginger. Use powdered ginger from the grocery store spice section or pound fresh ginger root from the produce section.
■ Juice squeezed from one-half of a lime.
■ Two and one-half cups sugar. Mix it well with a spoon until the sugar dissolves.
■ Three tablespoons cream of tartar. Mix well again.

2 Let the mixture cool to lukewarm. It is luke-warm when you put a drop on your wrist and it feels warm, but not hot. Ask your parents to show you how it is done. (Be careful. If the mixture is too hot, it will kill the yeast. It may also burn your wrist.) Once it's lukewarm, add 1 tablespoon baker's yeast and mix well. Cover the pot and let the mixture sit for six hours.

3 Now it is time to bottle your ginger ale. Start by straining it through a coffee filter or cheesecloth that's set into the top of a funnel. Some bits and pieces may slip through the cheese-cloth. That's okay. They will settle to the bottom. *Be sure to leave an air space at the top of the bottle to collect carbon dioxide.* Without the space, your jug may blow its top.

4 Once the ginger ale is in the jug, cap it tightly and put it into the refrig-erator. Make sure you keep your ginger ale in the refriger-ator. If it's not kept cool, the yeast will be very active mak-ing carbon dioxide and alcohol. Alcohol may be fine in some adult drinks, but it is not fine in ginger ale. It will give your ginger ale an unpleasant flavor.

5 You can drink your ginger ale right away, but it will taste better if you wait two days. When you take your ginger ale out of the refrigerator, look for the bubbles.

Watch them rise to the surface and release their carbon dioxide. *Slowly* unscrew the top of the jug. Listen for a slow fizzle and then a POP! when the gas escapes from the jug. What does your brew smell like? More important, how does it taste?

VARIATIONS

■ Give your ginger ale even more flavor by adding a cup of fresh, chopped mint leaves when you put the ginger in. Then just strain them out with the ginger.

■ Try using honey to replace the sugar called for in the experiment.

■ For another taste treat, add your homemade ginger ale to lemonade or fruit juices. Make up your own variations. With homemade ginger ale, creativity is always in good taste.

AFTERWORDS

Yeasts are very tiny plants. They are related to mushrooms, molds, and other fungi. Like other fungi, yeasts can't produce their own food. To get energy, yeasts must first break down sugars and other carbohydrates.

Yeasts take in sugar, a molecule high in energy, and break it down into carbon dioxide and alcohol. This process is called fermentation. Yeasts use the energy released from this breakdown to support their own life processes. A similar reaction occurs when campers set fire to a pile of wood to release heat.

Through research and breeding experiments scientists have learned to produce yeasts that can make especially large amounts of carbon dioxide and yeasts that can make especially large amounts of alcohol.

Bakers take advantage of yeast that makes high levels of carbon dioxide in bread-making. The gas bubbles that the baker's yeast gives off makes bread dough rise.

To make wine and beer, brewers use a yeast that produces high levels of alcohol. Since early times, brewer's yeast has also been used to cure various illnesses. It contains large amounts of B-complex vitamins that can be used by people. Baker's yeast does not.

The carbonation in your family's ginger ale results from the same reaction that occurs in your homemade bread or biscuits. Baker's yeast creates carbon dioxide that makes the bread dough rise. In the case of your ginger ale, the bottle cap keeps the carbon dioxide bubbles from escaping. They stay in the ginger ale solution, giving it that carbonated fizz.

Commercially made ginger ale goes through a different process. Instead of letting yeast make carbon dioxide bubbles, ginger ale manufacturers pump carbon dioxide into the ginger ale solution. The whole process is done under pressure, so that the gas bubbles are forced into the solution. The end product is the same—a fizzle when you open the bottle and bubbles of carbon dioxide you swallow when you drink ginger ale.

Yeasts contribute to the production of several other commercial food products. When fermentation is allowed to occur in the presence of oxygen, the yeast produces vinegar instead of alcohol. A poorly sealed bottle of wine may let oxygen into it, causing the wine to turn to vinegar. In the past, bacterial invasions into yeast doughs have resulted in new bread varieties. For instance, both rye and sourdough breads are made with a special "starter." The starter consists of the yeast dough combined with unique bacteria that gives a distinct flavor to each of these breads.

BOATS AFLOAT

BOATS AFLOAT

Planning an ocean voyage? Maybe you'd better take an hour to try this experiment before you set sail!

YOU WILL NEED

Plasticine or florist's clay
1 or 2 Large pots, pans, or basins
1 Pound of 1" finishing nails, or 2 or 3 dozen marbles all the same size, or box of paper clips
Cookie cutter or jar lid
1¼ Cups salt
2 Cups cooking oil
2 Bottle caps, 20" string, tape, long (1" or more) pin, plastic soda straw, 2 tall drinking glasses

Drop a steel nail into the water and it sinks right to the bottom. So how is it possible that a huge steel ship floats? You may think it has something to do with air trapped in compartments in the bottom of the ship. A little research will tell you if this is true or not.

1 Roll a piece of Plasticine or clay into a ball about the size of a golf ball. What happens when you drop the ball into a pot of water? Now take the ball and form it into a flat boat shape. Then take some small objects like nails, marbles, or paper clips and drop them in the boat. How many weights will your boat hold before it sinks? Now mold the same piece of Plasticine or clay into different boat shapes. What is the most any of these boats can hold and still float? What shape of boat seems to be able to carry the most?

2 Now organize a contest to see whose boat can carry the biggest load. Use a cookie cutter or jar lid to cut pieces of Plasticine or clay that are all the same size. Give each person a piece and have them build their own boats. Make up some contest rules. You'll have to decide when a loaded boat is still considered "floating": when it is halfway above the water, a quarter of the way, or just slightly under the water? Must the boat stay afloat for a minute or two after the last weight is added?

3 Try this contest: Who can build the smallest boat able to keep one marble afloat? You may need to make a balance to help you decide the winner of this contest. (See, Making a Balance, on this page.)

4 See how saltwater can affect your ships' ability to float. Mix 1¼ cups of salt with 1 quart of water (double these amounts if you need to). Let the saltwater stand for a while before you work with it. Meanwhile, float one boat in freshwater and write down how many weights it can carry. Then put the same boat in the saltwater. Does the number of weights change? (Saltwater can be rough on your hands, so use a plastic spoon to fish your boats and weights out.)

5 Now you've learned that the type of water itself works in helping boats float. But what would happen if you used 2 cups of cooking oil instead of water? How many weights can your boat carry then?

MAKING A BALANCE

1. Cut the 20" string in two. Cross the two 10" strings on top of a bottle cap and tape them in place. Turn the bottle cap over and pick up the four ends of the strings. Knot them together about 3" away from the cap. This is one *balance pan.*

2. Make another balance pan. Then hang one on each end of a plastic soda straw. Tape them in place. Push a long pin through the center, halfway down the straw. Stand two drinking glasses or jars close enough together so that the pin can rest on both rims and the balance can move freely. (Wiggle the pin back and forth a few times if the hole seems too tight.)

3. If your balance isn't exactly level when it is empty, stick bits of Plasticine or clay on the higher pan until it is level with the other. When you are trying to find out whose boat is smallest for Experiment Step 3, put a boat in each of the pans. When you see which is the lighter boat, leave it in one pan and set another boat in the second pan. Continue to weigh the boats against each other until you find the lightest one — the winner!

AFTERWORDS

Archimedes is probably the most famous bather of all time. He lived in Sicily more than 2,000 years ago and was a friend of the king. The king suspected that his new crown was not pure gold and asked Archimedes to investigate.

Archimedes could find out easily how much the crown weighed, but he didn't know how to calculate its *volume* (the amount of space it took up). As the story goes, Archimedes was lowering himself into his filled bathtub when he noticed the water spilling over the sides. Supposedly he was so excited by his discovery that he ran into the street yelling, *"Eureka!"* ("I have found it!" — the answer to his problem). He then dropped the crown into a full basin of water, catching the overflow. Next he weighed it against an equal volume of pure gold.

2 TALL DRINKING GLASSES — PIN

SALT
NAILS
SALT WATER
SALAD OIL
NAILS
PAPER CLIP
MARBLE
TAPE PAPER TO TOOTH PICK TO MAKE A SAIL

His demonstration for the king showed that the pure gold was heavier than the "gold" crown, thus proving that it had been mixed with a lighter, cheaper metal. Some detective work!

When a ship is lowered into water, it *displaces* the water, pushing it out of the way. It does this until the weight of the displacement equals the weight of the ship —and the ship floats. Remember how your ball of Plasticine or clay sank? But after you flattened it out and turned up the edges, it floated. The shape of the thinner hull was able to displace enough water to equal the weight of the Plasticine plus its load.

Up until about 100 years ago, a ship's owner could have loaded his vessel with as much as he pleased. Many overloaded ships and their crews were lost when the boats sank in storms at sea. Then, in 1876, Samuel Plimsoll persuaded the British government to pass a law to control the loading of ships. The law required that every ship be marked with a horizontal line on its side to show the safe loading limit.

C = Coastal Service
TF = Tropical Freshwater
T = Tropical
F = Freshwater
S = Summer
W = Winter
WNA = Winter North Atlantic
AB = American Bureau of Shipping (the authority that decides where the marks should be)

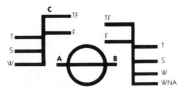

Notice that the Plimsoll marks also show the safe-loading limits for ships in different kinds of water and in different seasons. That's because, if you have two identical buckets and fill one with saltwater and the other with freshwater, the saltwater will weigh more. Saltwater is more *dense*, therefore heavier, than freshwater. Also, a bucket of warm saltwater from the Gulf of Mexico will weigh less than the same bucket filled with cold North Atlantic saltwater because cold water is more dense than warm water. Water temperatures also change according to the season.

Remember that a loaded ship floats because it displaces its own weight? Well, in dense waters (cold or saltwater), the ship won't sink as low into the water. In warm or non-salty waters, the ship has to displace *more* water in order to float. So, if an ocean vessel loses its way and happens to chug up the freshwater Mississippi River, it will sink lower into the water.

FLASH DANCE

FLASH DANCE

Put on your dancing shoes — it's time to *boogie!* All you need is a strobe to light up your life and help you catch all the flashiest action! It should take about 30 minutes to make.

YOU WILL NEED

Empty cardboard box, about 16″ by 16″ by 9″ or at least 2″ narrower than the length of your drill and bit
Pencil and compass for drawing a circle
Utility knife
Crank-type hand drill with ¼″ drill bit
Piece of cardboard from another box, 12″ by 12″
Scissors
Jumbo-size drinking straw
Masking tape
Ruler
Bright flashlight
Bicycle (optional)

Have you ever seen people dancing in the light of a flashing strobe? Their movements look jerky — like they're moving in slow motion. With a stroboscope, you can create all kinds of special visual effects. You can even make drops of water seem to *stop* in midair! Just get ready…turn out the lights…and do the Flash Dance!

1 To make your stroboscope, or strobe light, you will need to cut several holes in two sides of your cardboard box. Use the two biggest sides of the box and consider one side the "front" and the other the "back."

First, make a small hole with the point of your pencil in the front of the box. Position the hole about 3″ down from the top of the box, and cen-

DRILL HANDLE IN SLASH

tered between the corners. Then use a utility knife or scissors to cut a vertical opening in the *back* of the box, opposite the pencil hole. This vertical slash should start at the top of the box and be about 3″ long. Make the opening 1½″ wide — or wide enough so that the handle of your drill can sit in the space you've made. Be sure to center the slash between the corners of the box. Now you should be able to push the drill bit through the hole in the front, and rest the drill handle in the slash in the back of the box, as shown in the diagram.

2 Use a compass to draw a circle 12″ in diameter on the extra piece of cardboard and cut the circle out with scissors. Draw a line across the circle, through the

12″ DIAMETER

2″ x ½″ SLOTS

center hole, to mark the diameter. Cut two slots in the disk, on the diameter line, each starting about one inch from the edge of the circle. Each slot should be 2″ long and ½″ wide. With a pencil, poke a hole in the exact center of the disk. Make the hole just big enough to push the drinking straw through.

3 Cut off a piece of the straw, making it the same length as the drill bit. In one end of the straw, use scissors to cut 4 slashes, each about 1″ long. Now you should be able to bend the four split ends of straw backward, to use as tabs.

4 Push the straw through the hole in the disk, and bend the tabs flat

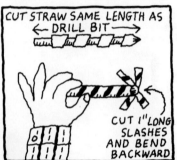

CUT STRAW SAME LENGTH AS ← DRILL BIT →

CUT 1″ LONG SLASHES AND BEND BACKWARD

against it. With masking tape, secure the tabs to the face of the disk. Remove the drill bit from the drill, and put the bit inside the straw, with the point of the bit going toward the tabs. Now the drill bit is inside the straw, and the straw is attached to the cardboard disk. Stick the straw-and-bit combo through the hole in the front of the carton. From inside the carton, tighten the straw-and-bit combo in the drill chuck — the place where the drill bit fits into the drill. If you have done this correctly, you will be able to turn the crank on the drill and see the disk spin around.

5 Next you will need to cut a square hole 2" by 2" on the front of the carton. *You must make*

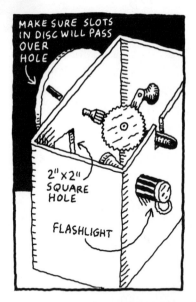

MAKE SURE SLOTS IN DISC WILL PASS OVER HOLE

2" X 2" SQUARE HOLE

FLASHLIGHT

sure that the slots in the disk will pass right over this hole as the disk turns. To mark the place, hold the disk still and make a line on the carton by drawing through one of the slots. Then cut through the mark with the utility knife. Now, working from the inside of the box, enlarge the hole around the cut you just made, so that the hole is 2" square.

6 Another hole must be made in the *back* of the box, exactly opposite the 2" square hole in the front

of the box. Make this last hole just big enough for your flashlight — so that the flashlight can be wedged tightly into the hole. The flashlight should shine directly through the 2" square hole in the front.

7 Now it's showtime! Turn out all the lights, and turn on the flashlight. When you rotate the disk by turning the drill crank, the light will shine out of the front of the box in flashes. The faster you turn the crank, the faster the strobe will flash.

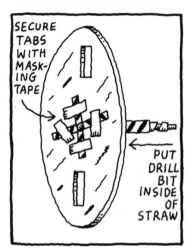

SECURE TABS WITH MASKING TAPE

PUT DRILL BIT INSIDE OF STRAW

ST/87

You may need a friend or two to help you experiment with your strobe. One person can hold the flashlight, to make sure the light is shining straight through the 2" square hole in the front. (Or balance the flashlight on some books set in the box.) Another person can turn the crank on the drill while you try these experiments:

■ Put on light-colored clothes and dance in the strobe-light beam! Can you figure out why your movements look jerky?

■ Turn on a water faucet so that the water comes out in a thin stream of droplets. Then turn out the lights and shine your flashing strobe at the water. Can you make the drops hang in space? Can you make the drops of water appear to move *upward*?

■ Turn your bicycle upside down and spin the front wheel. With all the lights out, shine your strobe at the spinning tire. If you vary the speed of the strobe light, you will be able to make the wheel appear to stop spinning. Can you make it look like the wheel is spinning backward? Can you use your strobe to figure out how fast (how many revolutions per minute) your bicycle tire is spinning?

■ Try using a slide projector, instead of a flashlight, as the light source in your stroboscope. The stronger beam of light will give you more dramatic effects.

AFTERWORDS

Did your stroboscope really make drops of water hang in midair—or were your eyes playing tricks? The answer is: both. Water *does* come out of the faucet drop by drop. But water moves so quickly that normally you can't look at just one drop: Another drop always comes along before you even get a chance to zero in on the first one! They all flow together in your mind, and in fact they all flow together as they come out of the faucet, too.

But—if you turned the crank of your stroboscope at just the right speed, the drop of water you looked at seemed to hang in midair. And as everyone knows, water drops don't do that; what you were really seeing was a series of drops of water. First you saw drop #1 suspended, let's say, about an inch below the faucet. Then the stroboscope turned out the light, and didn't turn it back on again until *another* drop of water—drop #2—was in that same position!

Then the light went out, and came back on again for drop #3. This created the illusion that one drop was hanging in midair, when really you were seeing many drops, each falling into the exact same position below the faucet.

By turning the crank even faster, perhaps you saw the drops of water appear to move up—back into the faucet! Here's what happened: First you looked at drop #1, an inch below the faucet. Then you look at drop #2, but it was only ¾" below the faucet. When the light came on again, drop #3 had fallen to only ½" below the faucet. Each drop you looked at was closer to the faucet, so the drops appeared to be going backward.

The stroboscope produces fabulous lighting effects, but the stroboscope business would probably flicker and die out if those were the only uses for this fancy flashing light. For instance, did you know that auto mechanics use strobe lights to work on your car engine? They use them to visually stop the action of the crankshaft, which is spinning around rapidly while the motor is running. That way they can check to see if the engine timing is accurate—in other words, they can make sure that everything is happening at just the right moment to make the car run smoothly.

Strobe lights also let mechanics in other industries view their machinery while it is in operation, to check for defects or to observe parts that might need adjustment. For instance, huge gears in factory equipment may appear to be meshing when the machine is turned off. But under the stress of operation, the gears could be coming together incorrectly. The only way to check it out is to look at the gears while the machine is running. Superstrobe to the rescue!

In the newspaper industry, strobes are used to visually "slow down" the huge rolls of paper that fly across the press. Pressmen can then read the newspapers *while* they are being printed, to make sure that the printing job is right. In the audio equipment industry, strobe lights are used to view the vibrating parts in a loudspeaker. And with flash strobe photography, biologists can record and study such things as the movements of a hummingbird's wings!

FANCY PLANTS

FANCY PLANTS

It'll take only 90 minutes to set up this activity, but you'll have to wait a week or two before your Fancy Plants take on the color of spring.

YOU WILL NEED

Scissors, pen
1 Sponge
A small plate
Grass seed or ryegrass
    seed, radish seeds,
    and mung beans
Plastic wrap, plastic bags
1 Styrofoam cup
Cotton balls
Paper towels
Empty egg carton, yogurt
    container, or similar boxes
Soil
Old shirt with pocket
Jar with a screw top
Black construction paper

Why do you think plants grow in the ground? And why *don't* they grow on park benches, or on tabletops, or on the roofs of parked cars? If your answer is "Plants need soil to grow in," you'll be surprised to find out that just isn't true! At least, it isn't *always* true. You can grow some plants — like grass, for instance — in sponges, on paper towels, and maybe even in a shirt! Use your imagination and come up with as many different Fancy Plants as you can.

1 Use a scissors to cut a sponge into a 1" wide snake shape. Soak the snake sponge in water, and put it on a small shallow plate. Carefully plant the sponge with grass seed, making sure you push some of the seeds into the holes in the sponge. Cover the plate with plastic wrap. Set the plate near a window. Keep the sponge wet, and watch for roots. Remove the plastic wrap when green appears. Water the snake-in-the-grass several times a day!

2 Now, let's see if this experiment works with other things. Draw a face on the outside of a Styrofoam cup. Fill the cup with cotton balls soaked in water. Sprinkle grass seed on top of the cotton balls and seal the whole cup in a plastic bag. When the green grass "hair" grows, remove the plastic bag and water the grass frequently.

3 Fill the sections of an empty egg carton with various soil substitutes, such as sand, crumpled tissues, tiny pebbles, sawdust, clean cat litter, loose tea, marbles, or whatever else you can think of. Fill one section of the egg carton with soil. This will be the "control" part of this experiment. Plant some radish seeds in each section of the egg carton. Water every day. What do you notice about the roots? Do the radishes grow better when you put the egg carton in a closet for the first few days? Which part of the plant grows better in the dark — the leaves or the roots?

4 Try planting some grass seed in the pocket of an old shirt. Hang the shirt on a hanger and water or mist it frequently. Seal it in a plastic bag until the grass sprouts.

5 Watch seeds grow by planting mung beans in a screw-top jar lined with a sheet of black construction paper. The seeds should go between the black paper and the jar. Fill the center of the jar with wet paper towels, and add ½" of water to the jar to keep the whole thing moist. Screw the lid on and lay the jar on its side. You'll be able to see roots and shoots growing against the black-paper liner within a week.

STAY IN CONTROL

With any science experiment, it's important that you, the scientist, remain in control. *You* must control the conditions of the experiment and *you* control the "variables" — the things that could change and affect the results of the experiment. That's why it's a good idea to have what scientists call the "control group" in your experiment. For instance, in Fancy Plants, you will plant grass seed in a sponge. But what if it doesn't grow? Is it

25

because the sponge isn't a good place for the seeds, or because there isn't enough warmth and light? Is there too much water, or not enough, in the sponge? The only way to find out for sure is to plant some of the same kind of grass seed in soil and take care of it in exactly the same way and at the same time as you do your experiment. This will be your control group. Set the control group in the same location with the seeded sponge. Water them both at the same time, with the same amount of water. Now you are in control of the experiment. If the grass planted in soil grows better than the grass planted in the sponge, you'll know that the sponge was the only reason for the difference in the results!

AFTERWORDS

As easy as it is to start grass or radishes in such unlikely places as a sponge or a shirt, these plants won't live long without constant attention and nurturing. You probably wouldn't want to spend the time it would take to keep your grass snake growing forever. But sometimes it *is* worthwhile to invest the extra time and technology needed to grow plants without soil. This method is called hydroponics. By looking at the techniques used in hydroponics, you'll discover why *soil* is such a perfect place for plants.

Water, air, light, warmth, nutrients, and stability. In just about that order, those are the things plants need to grow and thrive. With water at the top of the list, it's not surprising that some of the first experiments with soil substitutes involved using plain water as the growing medium. In fact, the word hydroponics comes from the Greek word for water. But, as early researchers soon found, there are a number of problems with trying to grow plants in a big tub of water.

The first problem is that water does not support a root system. To give plants stability, they must be suspended above the water tank by some sort of structure or base. Another problem is that water doesn't allow oxygen to flow freely to the roots. To cope with that deficiency, some hydroponic systems add air to the water with a motorized piece of equipment, a lot like the one you might use on a tropical fish tank. But then there's the question of nutrients. Elements like nitrogen, potassium, phosphorus, magnesium, and calcium are needed in relatively large amounts, and trace elements like iron, copper, and zinc are needed in tiny amounts. Water doesn't have a rich supply of these elements, and no matter how long the plants grow, the water won't be able to produce the nutrients or renew them over a period of time. They must be purchased and added in carefully controlled amounts, over and over again.

These drawbacks led many hydroponic growers to switch from just water to water and gravel as a growing medium, because gravel makes a sturdy base for the roots. But since gravel doesn't contain *any* nutrients and doesn't retain water, this method presents a whole new set of problems that must be overcome.

Now how does all of this compare with the time-honored method of growing plants in soil? Not too well. Without any supervision from the grower, *good* soil gives plants stability for their root systems. It also allows plenty of oxygen to reach the roots, and it contains most of the nutrients needed for growth. And unlike sand, gravel, loose tea, cat litter, sponges, and whatever else you might have experimented with in Fancy Plants, good soil can *hold onto* the water it receives for more than an hour. Generally speaking, good soil just naturally provides the things plants need.

But admittedly, not all soil is good soil. And in some parts of the world the time and expense needed to make the land ready for planting is overwhelming. In those regions, hydroponics is a "natural" choice — a way to supply locally grown crops at a lower cost.

JUST PLANE WINGS

JUST PLANE WINGS

Don't be a sore loser—be a *soaring* winner, with these paper airplanes that help you reach new heights. It will take you only a few minutes to make your airplanes, but you may want to test-fly them all day!

YOU WILL NEED

Several sheets of 8½" by 11" paper
Paper clips
Ruler
Scissors
Plastic straws

What one thing do jet fighters, bumblebees, bluejays, and paper airplanes all have in common? The answer is wings, of course. Wings are the one thing you've got to have if you're going to fly. But don't be surprised if some wings look a little bit different from others!

STUNT FLYER

This is the best paper airplane ever! It will loop-the-loop, do a barrel roll, or glide for long distances on a gentle breeze. And best of all, it has a snub nose, so you can zoom it at your friends without hurting anyone.

1 Start with an 8½" by 11" piece of paper. Fold it in half lengthwise, then open the paper up again. Bring the two top corners to meet on the middle fold, as in diagram 1. Then fold the top triangle down across line A-B, as in diagram 2.

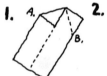

2 Fold up the point of the triangle, point C, so that it is about an inch long, as in diagram 3.

3 Now fold points A and B in toward the center line, so that they meet on top of the small triangle. They should touch the triangle a little less than halfway up from its fold. See diagram 4.

4 Bring the folded edges of the plane (line X and line Y on the diagram) to meet in the middle. Diagram 5 shows the airplane after one side has been folded in. The dotted line shows where the other side will be folded.

5 Now the paper airplane is ready to fly! Simply fold it in half lengthwise, along the center line, and hold the airplane from underneath. The snub-nosed end is the front, of course. Fly the airplane as it is a few times, and then add a paper clip just under the nose. Does your plane fly better with or without the paper clip? Where does the clip work best? When you try the stunts below, be sure to try them with and without the paper clip.

Stunts

■ To make your stunt plane do a barrel roll, bend or curl one tail piece *up* about an inch, and bend or curl the other tail piece *down* about an inch.

■ To loop-the-loop (your plane will curve down and come back to you), bend both tail pieces down. It may take some practice to throw the Stunt Flyer properly. If you want it to come right back to your hand, aim upward when you throw it.

■ The Stunt Flyer can loop-the-loop the opposite way—by curving up and around—and then it will keep on going! To do this stunt, bend both tail pieces up, and snap your wrist when you fly the plane. It will take some practice, but it's worth it!

HELICOPTER

This paper flyer moves just like the blades of a helicopter. Try making very small paper helicopters and very large ones. Stand on a chair and drop two different ones at the same time. Do they both descend at the same speed?

1 To make a paper helicopter, cut a strip of paper 11" long and 2" wide. Following the diagram, cut along the solid lines. There are only three cuts to be made. Cut #1 is 5" long, and the other two cuts are each about ⅔" long.

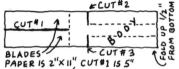

BLADES
PAPER IS 2"×11", CUT#1 IS 5"
(FOLD UP ½" FROM BOTTOM)

2 Now make the two long folds, along the dotted lines. These folds cause the body of the helicopter to be folded in thirds, with the two sides overlapping the center. Fold the bottom of the helicopter up a half inch and then

another half inch, to make the bottom heavier. You can also put a paper clip on the bottom to weight it.

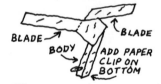

BLADE
BODY
BLADE
ADD PAPER CLIP ON BOTTOM

3 Last, fold the blades of the helicopter in opposite directions. One should point toward you and the other should point away.

4 Drop your helicopter from a high place, or stand on a chair and let it go. What makes it twirl? How is your helicopter different from a real helicopter? *Hint:* Can your helicopter ever go *up*?

WHIRLY TWIRLER

You can make a Whirly Twirler with only a drinking straw

and a small piece of paper.

1 Cut or tear a piece of paper to make a rectangle about 1½" wide and 6½" long. Fold the

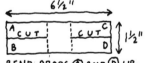

6½"

A CUT C
B CUT D

1½"

BEND PROPS Ⓐ AND Ⓓ UP.
BEND PROPS Ⓑ AND Ⓒ DOWN.

paper in half lengthwise. Cut or tear along the fold from each end toward the middle, leaving the center of the paper untorn. Now you have

DROP YOUR HELICOPTER FROM A HIGH PLACE

HELI-COPTER

four propellers.

2 Bend one propeller up and the other down on one side of the paper. Bend the opposite propellers up and down on the other side of the paper, as shown in the diagram.

POKE STRAW THRU CENTER

3 Poke the straw through the center of the paper and your Whirly Twirler is done! Let it fall from a high place and see whether it spins faster or slower than the paper helicopter.

SUPER LOOPS

For this amazing glider, you need one plastic straw and two strips of paper, each 1¼" wide.

STUNT FLYER →

SUPER LOOPS

WHIRLY TWIRLER

ROCKET BOMBER

ST/88

1 Cut one paper strip 7" long and the other strip 9" long. Make the strips into loops by overlapping the ends about an inch or so and taping them closed.

TAPE LOOPS TO STRAW

2 Next tape the loops to the straw, as shown. Where are the wings? To fly this plane, hold it with the smaller loop facing forward, and the straw on the bottom. It will glide and sometimes even spiral as it soars across your living room.

ROCKET BOMBER

Can a rolled-up piece of notebook paper fly? Try it and find out.

1 Take an 8½" by 11" sheet of paper and roll it into a tube with a 1" diameter. Use tape to keep it closed. Try to fly it across the room.

2 Now roll up another piece of paper the same way and tape it closed. Cut a 2" slash in one end. Cut sideways from the slash in two directions, so that a tail is formed, as in the diagram.

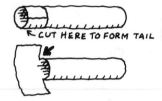

CUT HERE TO FORM TAIL

3 Fly the Rocket Bomber with the tail toward the back. Does the Rocket Bomber have wings? Do real rockets have wings? Do they have tails?

AFTERWORDS

For thousands of years, people have wanted to be able to fly like the birds. But have they succeeded? Technically, no! Even today, no one has mastered the art of flying the way birds do: by flapping their wings.

Flapping wings are unique to birds, although many people have tried— and failed—to imitate them. Still scientists dreamed of flight for many years. Leonardo da Vinci made a drawing of a design for a helicopter—almost 500 years before it was invented! And Sir Isaac Newton understood the principles of flight, but he ended up predicting that people would never fly!

Modern scientists have studied the flapping motion of birds' wings, and found out just how tricky flapping flight is. For one thing, a bird's wing does not merely go up and down in two evenly timed movements. The downward motion is smooth and slow, while the upward motion is faster and includes a flicking motion. If you watch a bird flying, you'll notice that it's easier to see the wings' downbeat, because it lasts longer.

Although no one has mastered flapping flight, airplanes do glide and soar using some of the same design elements found on birds. An airplane's wings are curved at the front and tapered at the back, like a bird's. And flaps on an airplane wing can be moved up or down to increase the curvature of the wing during takeoff and landing. Those adjustments are similar to the changes you made when you changed the position of the tail pieces on your paper airplane. Of course you can only make a *few* adjustments in the wings or tail pieces of your paper flyers, compared with the *hundreds* of tiny adjustments that birds make.

Another similarity between birds, planes, and paper airplanes is the need for a tail. The tail is used for steering and for balance. Without a tail, birds and planes would tend to go topsy-turvy and take an unscheduled nose dive. That's probably what happened to your Rocket Bomber when it was just a paper tube without a tail.

Whether you're flying a paper Stunt Flyer or a DC-10 commercial jet, the principles of flight remain the same. The airplane must go fast enough to create something called *lift*. Lift is the result of air flowing over the wings of a plane at a great speed. The air pressure above the wing is less than the air pressure below the wing, so the plane goes up. Why can't your paper airplane just glide on forever? Because it doesn't have a motor... and as it starts to slow down, the air pressure above the wing increases. No more lift— and no more flight!

FOR THE BIRDS

FOR THE BIRDS

You don't need to take out an ad in the *Bird Gazette* to let the birds in your neighborhood know that you care! Just put out a bird feeder. It will take about 30 minutes to make a simple feeder. Then you can watch the action for hours.

YOU WILL NEED

Empty milk carton, soda bottle, or bleach bottle
Duct tape or other heavy, waterproof tape
Scissors or knife
Pipe cleaners
Popsicle sticks
Colored paper for decorating feeder
Glue
Rope or clothesline
Birdseed

In winter, the insects, seeds, and berries that songbirds eat are scarce, and snow often covers the ground. Many birds will starve or freeze if they don't find enough food to eat. You can make a bird feeder and put it in your yard, in a park, or out along the roadside, to help feed the winter birds. Do it now, because that way the birds will learn to come to your feeder before the cold weather arrives. And keep your feeder filled into the spring, because the birds have learned to count on you for food!

If you live in a warmer part of the country, you're lucky. Many songbirds are there all year round. Having a bird feeder is a great way to meet them!

1 Wash out an empty 1-quart milk carton, a 2-liter soda bottle, and/or an empty bleach bottle with a handle. *Be sure the container is well rinsed before you begin.*

2 Seal the original opening with duct tape. If you are using a milk carton, close it and tape the top tightly shut. If you are using a plastic bottle, screw the cap on tightly and seal with duct tape. Remove any labels from the bottle.

3 With your scissors, cut a small door or opening in the container about 5 inches from the bottom. There are lots of ways to construct a feeder. If you are using a soda bottle, you can lay it on its side and call that the bottom. In that case, you might want to make two doors. They can open sideways, like a door, or upwards, like a tent flap. Make the doors small if you want to discourage larger birds: Large birds sometimes scare the smaller birds away. If you make a huge hole in your feeder, you'll probably end up feeding squirrels instead!

4 Tie the door open with a pipe cleaner. Put a small hole in the door and a small hole in the feeder. Put a pipe cleaner through the hole in the door and knot it or twist it. Put the other end through the hole in the bottle and knot it.

5 Make a perch for the birds to stand on when they come to your bird feeder. You will need two Popsicle sticks for each perch. Use scissors or a knife to make a small slit about ½" below the opening in the feeder. Make another slit about ½" below the first slit. Push one Popsicle stick through each slit until only about 2" of each stick remains outside the feeder. Tape the two sticks together with duct tape to form a wedge-shaped perch. (If using a milk carton, also decorate the outside of your feeder: Glue on some colored paper.)

6 You will need to make handles or straps to hang up your bird feeder. Where you put the handles will depend on what style of feeder you designed. For a bleach-bottle bird feeder, you can simply put a rope through the handle and suspend it from a tree branch. For a soda bottle turned on its side or for a milk carton, you will need two pipe-cleaner handles—one at each end of the top of your feeder. Poke two holes in the top left side of your feeder and push one pipe cleaner through both of them. Twist the ends together or knot them. Do the same at the right end of the top.

7 Fill your bird feeder with seeds. Make sure the birdseeds come all the way up to the opening, so that small birds can reach them—without having to climb *into* the bottle.

8 Make two or more feeders and find out which kind the birds like best. Do they want to be able to see the seeds inside? Or are they more attracted to a colorfully decorated bird feeder? Even if you made two bird feeders, use the same kind of birdseed in each one. That way you will know that it is the difference in shape or color of the bottle—and not the food inside—that explains why birds do or don't come to each feeder. Later, you can experiment with different kinds of food.

WHERE TO HANG YOUR BIRD FEEDER

Bird feeders should be hung at least 5 feet from the ground, so that dogs and cats cannot reach the birds while they are feeding. You'll also want to hang the feeder away from bushes or benches, so that squirrels cannot jump to the bird feeder and eat all the food. Suspend the feeder from a wire attached to a tree limb…or hang it from a clothesline.

WHAT TO FEED THE BIRDS

What do birds like to eat? Different birds like different kinds of seed. Many birds will also eat bread crumbs, fruits, nuts, and suet (beef fat). This list will help you decide what kind of food to use.

Bread Crumbs: Scatter fresh white bread crumbs (or small pieces of white bread) on the ground to attract birds.

Black-striped Sunflower Seeds: These seeds will attract bluejays, chickadees, grosbeaks, tufted titmice, finches, and cardinals.

Mixed Seeds: This is the most easily available kind of birdseed.

Fruits: Put out some raisins, apple slices, pieces of banana, and orange slices, especially in summer.

Suet: This beef fat is available in the grocery store. It will attract woodpeckers, which eat insects in summer.

Roasted Peanuts (in the shell): These are good for bluejays.

USE **2** POPSICLE STICKS TO MAKE PERCH

DECORATE MILK CARTON

HANG FEEDERS AT LEAST **5** FEET FROM GROUND

BIRD SEED

USE PIPE CLEANERS TO HANG FEEDERS WITHOUT HANDLES

ST/88

Peanut Butter: Plain peanut butter is too thick for birds to swallow. Use 1 cup of cornmeal to every ¼ cup of peanut butter. Add enough vegetable shortening to make it less sticky. You can smear the mixture directly on a tree trunk, or on a pinecone and hang it from a tree.

Water: Birds need water, so put out a saucer for them, or fill one of your extra feeders with water and cut a larger opening. Change the water frequently.

Grit: Mix a little sand or grit in with your birdseed. Birds must have grit to digest their food. They also like crushed eggshells for the calcium they contain.

CARE FOR YOUR FEEDER

Don't let the birdseed in your feeder get wet, soggy, or moldy. Birds can get a deadly disease from eating wet birdseed. Clean out the feeder and scrub it well about once a week—or make a new feeder with another soda bottle. It's easy!

AFTERWORDS

Have you ever heard someone say, "You're eating like a bird?" They probably meant that you weren't eating much. But birds actually eat quite a lot. In fact, most songbirds will eat many times a day—especially in winter, when they need the extra fuel to keep warm. And birds getting ready to migrate can double their own body weight in only a few days! They store up fat to use as fuel for their journey south.

But if adult birds eat a lot, baby birds eat *more,* especially just before they leave the nest. They must be fed *every 15 to 30 minutes* during the first few weeks of life! Their parents spend the whole day flying back and forth to the nest, bringing food. The baby that stretches its neck up the farthest and opens its mouth the widest is always fed first. That's just nature's way of making sure the hungriest bird gets what it needs.

Birds have excellent eyesight, which is how they find food. Did birds come to feed more quickly at your clear plastic soda-bottle feeder than at your less-transparent feeders? That's because they spotted the food from the air.

Of course, not all birds eat seeds, but birds of prey such as vultures and eagles also rely on their eyesight to lead them to food. Some owls' and eagles' eyes are actually larger than human eyes, and hawks are thought to see *10 times* better than human beings. Birds have superior vision for a number of reasons. They have a double set of muscles so they can focus more easily on objects at different distances. They also have more cones and rods—the cells in the eye that are sensitive to color and light.

If you're not sure what a certain species of bird eats, you can often figure it out by looking at the bird's beak. Each beak shape is suited to a specific purpose: For instance, the hooked bill of a hawk is used for striking and killing prey animals. The woodpecker's pointed bill is used to dig insects out of trees. The cone-shaped beak found on many songbirds can crack open or crush seeds. And the long, tapered bill of the hummingbird is perfect for reaching deep into flowers and sucking out nectar.

Although seed-eating birds have no teeth, they do need to grind up their food, the way animals and people do when they chew. That's why these birds eat grit—sand or small pebbles. This gravel stays in the bird's stomach, or *gizzard.* When the digestive muscles go to work, grinding and mashing up the food, the gravel acts like a hard, grinding surface.

What do songbirds eat when people aren't feeding them? In summer, many birds eat seeds and berries that are plentiful then. The seeds from pine trees are one of their most important sources of food. They eat the berries from almost every kind of bush imaginable, and also like acorns and cherries. Most important of all, many birds eat insects. If it weren't for birds, the world would be overrun with insects! Some farmers and gardeners put up bird feeders to attract these insect-eaters. The birds then take up residence in the area and help to control the insects that would otherwise do a lot of damage to crops.

Thanks to birds, the balance of nature is maintained. And thanks to your bird feeder, many birds will live through a cold winter.

MUD PIES

MUD PIES

Ummmm, delicious! A nice big plate of mud! Take about 30 minutes to dig the hole and plant the seeds. Wait 1 to 1½ weeks for them to sprout and find out who likes mud pies better — plants or kids!

YOU WILL NEED

4 Aluminum pie pans (disposable)
Shovel to dig soil, or large bag of potting soil
Pencil
Paper
Transparent tape
Nail
Popcorn kernels
Water
Large plate
A brick or piece of sandstone
Paper bag
Hammer
Dried-up modeling clay
Dried leaves, roots, and twigs
Food scraps such as carrot peelings, bread crumbs, and eggshells
Sand

What could be mushier, squishier, and gushier than a nice big mud pie! But plants are usually found in rich soil — not mud. What's the difference between mud and soil? Make your own mud pies and find out. And while you're waiting for your garden pies to sprout, you can also find out how long it takes nature to "make" soil out of the things that go into it.

1 If you can get permission to dig in your yard or somewhere in your neighborhood — great! Go outside and dig a hole about 18" deep. Take enough soil from the hole to completely fill 3 aluminum pie pans. Make sure the soil doesn't have plants already growing in it. (If you are digging in a grassy area, throw the grassy part away, and use the dirt below the grass roots.) Put soil from near the top of the hole — the topsoil — into two of the pie pans. Put soil from the bottom of the hole — the subsoil — into the third pie pan. Label the first two pies "Topsoil" and the

third pie "Subsoil."

If you can't find a place to dig, use potting soil from a garden shop for this activity. Fill *only one* pie pan with potting soil and label it "Soil without drainage holes." Then go on to Step 2.

2 Use a nail to punch about 20 to 30 holes in the bottom of an empty aluminum pie pan. Fill this pie pan with topsoil transferred from one of the other two pans, or use potting soil. For this pie, make a new label that says "Soil with drainage holes."

3 Sprinkle 1 or 2 tablespoons of unpopped popcorn kernels on each mud pie. Mix the popcorn into the dirt, so that the kernels are underneath the soil. Now water each of the three pies thoroughly, but first put the pie with drainage holes on a large plate to catch the water that drips out. Set all three mud pies in a sunny place. Water them often enough to keep the mud pies muddy — but do not *overwater* the one with drainage holes.

Which pie is the first one to sprout? Does the popcorn grow better in the subsoil mud pie, in the topsoil mud pie, or in the topsoil pie with drainage holes? What do you think plants in the pie with drainage holes get that they don't get in the mud pie that is constantly soaked with water?

4 While you're waiting for your mud pies to turn into popcorn pies, try making some soil of your own! First you will need to "weather," or break down, some rocks. Since you don't have a million years and an ocean full of water to do this, you'll have to use a hammer instead. Take a brick or large piece of sandstone outdoors and put it in a paper bag on the ground. Through the bag, hammer the brick or stone until it crumbles into tiny pieces. Put the crushed rock into an empty pie pan.

Do the same thing with a dried-up piece of clay. Hammer it until it is powdery and add it to the crushed rocks. Add some dried leaves and grass, dead bugs, roots, vegetable scraps, a little bit of sand, and then water the whole thing. Use just enough water to keep the contents moist, but not soupy. Stir up the pie. Now let your pie stand for — how long? A week? A month? How long will it take to make soil? Mix the pie up every few days, and sprinkle with water if it dries out completely. Even if it never really looks like soil, try planting popcorn in it to see what happens.

AFTERWORDS

The story of soil is a long one, starting back to when the Earth's crust was first cooling. There was no soil or dirt then—just rock. But over a period of thousands of years, little bits and pieces of rock were broken off. Some rocks were worn down by the rain and wind. Others were dissolved by acids in the water of lakes and oceans. And many huge boulders were cracked again and again—into smaller and smaller pieces—by the changes in temperature from freezing winter to scorching summer.

But crushed rocks aren't the only ingredient in soil. You also need water, oxygen, and *organic material*, which is what we call things that either *are* alive or *were* alive. So here comes the big question: Where did organic material, like plants for instance, come from if there wasn't any soil to grow them in?

Scientists think that life began in the oceans and crept slowly toward land. It took eons for the tiny bacteria and protozoa of the water to evolve into forms of life that could survive on land. Step by step, inch by inch, larger life-forms developed. When they died, they became the raw material to form soil, which in turn became a good place for even larger plants to grow.

Dead plants and animals are important ingredients of the soil, but *live* plants and animals play a primary role, too. Take worms, for instance. Without worms, many of the dead leaves from plants and crops would just lie there on top of the field, or be blown away. But earthworms take little bits of dried leaves with them down into the earth as they tunnel around. One scientist found that the worms in a 3-foot-square area could take as much as 20 pounds of dead leaves underground in just six months time!

In moist soils, earthworms are numerous. In some parts of the world, there are 2 million earthworms per acre! An average acre, though, would only have about 50,000 worms in it, all working to mix up the soil. Their burrowing also brings minerals from the layers of subsoil *up* to the topsoil. And their movement opens up air passages and keeps the soil loose so that water can enter the ground and plant roots can grow more easily. Other animals that live underground—such as moles, ants, and beetles—do the same job. But what turns the dead leaves and insects into soil?

Bacteria are microscopic plants that are present everywhere on Earth. If you thought there were a lot of earthworms in an acre, just think of this: As many as 50 *billion* bacteria are in one drop of water! A rule in science says that the smaller an organism is, the more of them you'll find—and the greater an effect they'll have on the environment. That law is definitely true when it comes to bacteria.

Bacteria perform two main jobs in helping to make soil and keeping the soil "healthy" so that plants can grow. First, bacteria cause dead plants and animals to *decompose*, or break down into simpler elements. Without bacteria, dead things wouldn't rot or decay. Second, a gas in the soil called *nitrogen* is essential for all living things. Some bacteria are called nitrogen "fixers," which means they help plants to use the nitrogen present in the soil.

So the next time you want to make mud pies, go right ahead. But do it with a little respect! After all: It took the earth a long time to produce that beautiful black stuff you call mud!

NIGHT MOVES

NIGHT MOVES

The first game in Night Moves can be played in 30 minutes or less. The second game is enough fun to fill up several hours on a steamy summer night. Just be sure to listen for the screech of a bat or the hoot of an owl whoooo might want to join in your experiment!

YOU WILL NEED

Clean laundry, especially socks
Paper and pen or marker
1 Piece of lightweight cardboard
Tape
Flashlight
Blindfold (optional)
A small empty can

Owls, bats, raccoons, deer, skunks, mice, and porcupines all get around in the dark very well. That's because they're all nocturnal animals, which means that they're up all night and they sleep all day. *You* may live that way sometimes, too — especially in the sum-mer. But that doesn't mean you're really adapted to the night the way nocturnal animals are. For one thing, you don't have the sharp hearing and keen eyesight that nocturnal animals have. And you probably don't need them. After all, you don't have to fight off vicious animals to get a decent snack during a late-night raid on the refrigerator!

But, hey — why feel inferior to these nighttime prowlers when you haven't even tested yourself in the dark? By playing these two games and making some Night Moves, you can find out just how different you and the wildlife are!

GAME No. 1:
SEEING IN THE DARK

1 Have ready a pile of clean, unsorted socks and a few shirts. Turn out all the lights in the room and close the blinds so that just a *little* light from the street comes in.

2 Look around the dark-ened room and talk about which things you can see clearly and which things you cannot see. Can you read a book title in the dark from 12 inches away? Have someone stand on the far side of the room, and hold up a shirt. Can you identify who it belongs to right away? Just wait…your eyes may not have completely adjusted to the dark.

3 Start sorting through the clean socks and take turns deciding what color each sock is. Put all the blue socks in one pile, all the red ones in another pile, and so on. Use the paper and pen or marker to make a sign labeling each pile of socks by color. Do you find yourself holding each sock up very close to your face to see the color better? Why do you think that is?

4 When you're finished sorting the socks, look around the room again. You'll notice that you can see much more now than you could when you'd only been in the dark for five minutes. Can you read the book title now?

5 Turn on the lights and check out the piles of socks. Most likely, you'll find some red socks in the black pile or some gray ones in the beige pile. And you might even find some things that aren't socks in the sock pile! As a matter of fact, maybe you should have a raccoon sort your laundry from now on!

GAME No. 2:
HEARING IN THE DARK

1 Use a lightweight piece of cardboard to make a cone with a 1" open-ing at the small end. Tape the cone over the end of a flashlight. This will narrow the beam of the flashlight so that the light shines on a smaller area.

2 Go outside after dark, or turn out all the lights in your living room, and choose someone to be "It." If you are playing this game outside, try to find a grassy spot to play it in. Have the person who is It sit down on the ground, either blindfolded or with his or her eyes closed, and let him or her hold the flashlight. Place an empty can a few feet behind the person who is It.

3 Have all the other players stand about 10 to 15 feet in front of the person who is It. These players are called the Creepers.

As quietly as possible, the Creepers must try to sneak past the person who is It.

4 Whenever the person who is It hears a Creeper coming, he or she points the flashlight in the direction of the sound and turns it on. Sweeping the flashlight back and forth is not allowed. If the flashlight beam actually shines on the Creeper, the Creeper must say "You got me," and go back to the starting line. But if the light doesn't touch the Creeper, then the Creeper may stay there, remain silent, and creep again. The person who is It should not remove the blindfold or open his or her eyes until the end of the game.

WHAT ARTICLE OF CLOTHING IS THIS?
TURN OUT THE LIGHTS!
CAN YOU READ THIS BOOK?
#1
NIGHT MOVES
CAN A CAT SEE BETTER THAN YOU?
WHAT COLOR IS THIS?

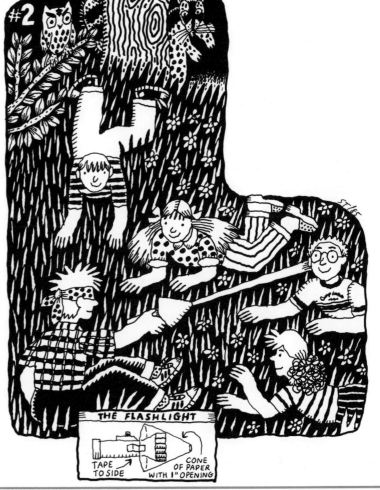

#2
THE FLASHLIGHT
TAPE TO SIDE
CONE OF PAPER WITH 1" OPENING

5 When all the Creepers have made it to the empty can behind the person who is It without getting caught in the flashlight beam, the game is over. Then it is someone else's turn to be It.

VARIATIONS

■ Play the game in a wooded spot; the leaves on bushes and the twigs on the ground will make it much harder to sneak around quietly.
■ Have the person who is It cover one ear during the game. Can he or she still tell where the creeping sounds are coming from? Do you think you need both ears to accurately sense the direction of sounds?
■ Set a limit on the number of times the flashlight may be turned on.

Now that you've played both games, what do you think about nocturnal animals? If you were an animal, would you rather have excellent night vision or terrific hearing?

AFTERWORDS

More than half of the world's animals are active at night. Considering how hard it is to get around in the dark, and how much easier it is to do things in daylight, the big question is: Why? Why are so many animals either nocturnal, which means they are active *only* at night, or arrhythmic (without rhythm), which means they can be just as active at night as they are in the daytime? Scientists believe the answer to that question has to do with the relationship between the predatory, or "hunting," animals and the animals that are their prey, the "hunted."

Here's how the theory goes. Long ago, when the animals we know today were first evolving, the prey animals found that if they wandered around in the daytime looking for food, they were easily seen by the predators, who quickly attacked. So the prey animals remained still during the day, whether they were sleeping or not. When the protective night came, they went looking for food. But in the dark, the animals needed excellent night vision and superior hearing to find a decent meal for themselves and still avoid becoming someone else's dinner. Within each species, a few animals *did* have superior senses and they survived the longest, passing their traits along to their offspring. Meanwhile, the predatory animals were staying up at night, too, and over time they developed the same good hearing and night vision as well. So they're all back to where they started!

With many animals, you can tell just by looking at them whether they have good night vision, supersensitive hearing, or both. All you have to do is observe the size of their ears and eyes. Big ears, which cup forward like a bell or a horn, "catch" more sound waves and direct them down into the animal's inner ear. Big eyes allow more light to enter the eye and strike a light-sensitive membrane called the retina. But even animals with small ears or small eyes can often see and hear better than people can, because the internal structure of their sense organs is so highly developed.

Consider the difference between a nocturnal animal's retina and yours, for example. Both types of retinas are made up of two different kinds of cells that can receive light. These cells are called *rods* and *cones*. Because they are much more sensitive to light, rods function in the dark or at night. Cones function during the day or in bright light because they are less sensitive. But a nocturnal animal's retina has many more rods than yours does. There may be as many as one million tightly packed rods to every $\frac{1}{25}$ of an inch of retina! That's why most nocturnal animals can see things in the dark that people aren't ever aware of.

But even if you had as many rods in your retina as an animal does, you still wouldn't be able to see colors in the dark. That's because rods aren't sensitive to color at all. Only cones are sensitive to color. When you played Night Moves, you weren't supposed to be able to sort the socks correctly — and if you *could*, it's because you had enough light in the room to stimulate the cones in your retina.

A MATTER OF TASTE

A MATTER OF TASTE

Most people love to eat! Part of the fun in eating depends on how food tastes. Can you imagine a hot dog without mustard or relish? Boring! These taste treats should take about an hour.

EXPERIMENT No. 1: MAPPING YOUR TONGUE

All of our tastes can be put into 4 main groups: *sweet* (sugar or honey or molasses), *sour* (lemons or limes or vinegar), *salty* (table salt) and *bitter* (baking chocolate or instant coffee). Your taste-tester — your tongue — can be grouped into 4 parts, too. Here's how.

YOU WILL NEED

Salt
Sugar
Vinegar
Instant coffee
Large paper cups
Small paper cups
Cotton swabs (Q-Tips)
Paper and pencil
Mirror
Blindfold (handkerchief or scarf)

1 Look in a mirror and stick out your tongue. Make a sketch of your tongue that looks like this. Make it about as big as the palm of your hand.

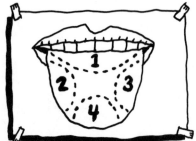

2 You will need separate solutions of salt, sugar, vinegar, and instant coffee. Put 2 level teaspoons of each substance into half a cup of water and stir. These are your "stock solutions"; label them. Next, label 4 smaller cups and pour a teaspoon of each stock solution into the proper cup. Put a cotton swab in each cup.

3 Blindfold a friend and tell him/her to stick out his/her tongue. Then take the swab out of one of the smaller cups, but don't tell your friend which one. Gently touch this swab to your friend's tongue in region 1. What does your friend taste when the swab first touches the tongue: sweet, like sugar; sour, like vinegar; salty, like table salt, or bitter, like coffee?

4 Record your friend's answer by writing one of the following symbols on your sketch of a tongue: "SW" for sweet; "SR" for sour; "SA" for salty; and "B" for bitter.

5 Do the same thing on regions 2, 3, and 4 (in that order). Then have your friend rinse the mouth with clean water and spit it out into another big paper cup. Repeat step 3 for each of the other 3 solutions.

6 Repeat testing all 4 solutions at least one more time, but the more times the better. Test other people, but be sure to use clean cups and swabs for each subject you test. Which parts of the tongue seem to be best for tasting each of the 4 tastes? How much do the taste regions overlap?

EXPERIMENT No. 2: NAME THAT TASTE

Now use your trusty tongue to see if it can identify different kinds of foods — even if you can't see or smell them!

YOU WILL NEED

Some different hard fruits and vegetables (such as potato, pear, apple, carrot, onion, squash, radish, turnip, parsnip, rutabaga, broccoli stem, cauliflower stem, sweet potato, or whatever other foods like these you have at home)
Paring knife
Paper cups
Toothpicks
Blindfold

1. Peel each of the fruits and vegetables, and cut them up into little pieces about the size of the eraser on a pencil. Put each food in a separate cup and label the cup.

2. Blindfold your friend and tell him/her to pinch his/her nose shut. Then use a clean toothpick to feed your friend a small piece of one of the foods. What does your friend think the food is?

3. Keep a record of your friend's guess by writing down the name of the food and putting a + beside it if he/she gets it right. (You may want to write down what he/she *thought* it was, if they don't guess right.)

4. Have your friend rinse his/her mouth with clear water between tests of each of the foods, so there's no leftover taste on the tongue. How many foods did your friend guess correctly?

5. Repeat steps 2, 3, and 4, but this time don't have the nose pinched shut. How many did your friend guess correctly this time? How does your sense of smell affect your sense of taste? Repeat all steps with another friend, but don't forget to use a clean toothpick with your next customer.

VARIATIONS

- Try feeding your blind-folded partner a piece of apple while you hold a piece of pear (or onion) close under his/her nose. What does he/she think is being eaten?
- Suck an ice cube for a few minutes. How do things taste when your tongue is cold?
- Pinch a copper penny, sandwiched by a small piece of aluminum foil, between your thumb and first finger. Touch the free ends of the two metals (the edge where the foil was cut) to the tip of your tongue. How does it taste?
- How well can you tell the taste of sugar solution from artificial sweeteners? (Try the regular brand of some pop and the diet brand of the same pop.) Which one do ants and flies go for?
- Repeat Experiment No. 2 but this time don't use a blind-fold or pinch your nose. Put some potato in a blender, add some green food coloring (Happy St. Patrick's Day?), and mix well. Do the same with other light-colored foods, like pear, apple, radish, turnip. How does color affect your sense of taste? Your enjoyment of food?

AFTERWORDS

What does rotten meat have to do with the discovery of America? Well, back in the time of Columbus there were no refrigerators, so fresh meat spoiled very quickly and smelled and tasted "bad." But even spoiled meat was too valuable to throw away, so people started to add spices and herbs to hide the rotten taste. These seasonings had to be brought from the Far East and Africa and this made them expensive. Columbus was looking for a quick way to the Far East when he bumped into America.

How do you like your chili? Hot? The sense of taste varies from person to person. Stick out your tongue and look at it in the mirror. You will see bumps and ridges between them. Within these bumps there are thousands of tiny *taste buds*. These are specialized cells connected by sensory nerves to your brain. When chemicals (food) are dissolved in the liquid on the surface of your tongue, they stimulate the taste buds and the nerves carry the message to the brain. Your brain then lets you know what you are tasting. There are 4 kinds of taste cells, one for each of the main tastes. Taste buds for sweet things are mostly located at the tip of your tongue. You taste most bitter things with taste buds at the back of your tongue. Sour and salty things are mostly picked up by taste buds on the edges of your tongue.

If you touch a penny or a piece of aluminum foil to your tongue, you feel a taste that is not caused by food. In this case, your taste buds are electrically stimulated by a *weak* electric current that is produced by the two different metals and your saliva. (Don't try this with any other kinds of electricity!)

How do things taste when your nose is stuffed up with a cold? Much of what we taste has to do with our sense of smell. In great-grandmother's time a favorite medicine was Castor Oil. It smelled rotten. Whenever she gave some to a child, she would pinch the child's nose shut. How good an idea was this? What part of your tongue should you avoid if you ever have to take bitter medicine?

You can tell right away if a food is too salty. But you may find that a piece of lemon doesn't taste sour until you actually bite down on it and some juice comes out. How well and how quickly you can taste something depends upon how well it dissolves in the liquid on your tongue. Salt dissolves very quickly. Solid lemon does not dissolve as quickly as lemon juice.

How do you like your pizza, hot or cold? Most people prefer hot foods because they seem to taste better. For one thing, hot foods give off more odors, which help to pep up your sense of taste. Warm foods also help to stimulate your taste buds. What happens to your sense of taste after you suck on an ice cube for a while?

Long ago, rich people and rulers, like kings and queens, were afraid that someone might try to poison them, so they would hire "official tasters" to sample food before it was eaten. Even today there are professional "tasters" who taste various blends of tea or wines to get the "blend" of several different tea leaves or wine grapes just right. What a tasty way to make a living!

KALEIDOSCOPE

KALEIDOSCOPE

For at least 150 years, kaleidoscopes have been turning out many beautiful patterns. With two mirrors and some bits of plastic, you can create some colorful images of your own in about 1 hour.

YOU WILL NEED

2 or 3 Identical mirrors, any size between 1½" to 3" wide and 6" to 12" long (You can get these from a glass shop; tell the salesperson what you are making and ask to have the mirrors' edges polished. If the glass shop doesn't polish the edges of the mirrors, you will also need some fine sandpaper, emery cloth, or an emery board, and a small block of wood.)
Glass cleaner
Tissues
Pencil
Ruler
Some strips of cardboard larger than your mirrors
Scissors
Black construction paper or black tempera paint
Quick-drying glue
Masking tape
1 Clear plastic notebook divider or a clear plastic food container lid
Scraps of colored plastic or unwanted color film slides, or confetti
1 Translucent food container lid (one that you can see light through, but you can't see through completely)

MAKE A "V" USING TWO MIRRORS

1" LINE

1 Safety first! If the edges of your mirrors are not polished, handle them *very carefully* and polish them yourself. Wrap some fine sandpaper or emery cloth around a small block of wood and *carefully* sand the sharp edges and corners. Or you can use an emery board (you won't need the wood block) to do the same thing. When the edges are smooth and safe enough to be handled, clean the mirrors with glass cleaner.

2 Now, before you make your kaleidoscope, try these mirror experiments to find out how kaleidoscopes work. Draw a line about 1" long on a piece of paper. Stand your two mirrors on their edges and make a "V" shape around the line, with one end of the line touching the point of the "V," as shown. What seems to happen to the line? Stand a pencil at the other end of the line. How many images of the pencil can you see? Change the angle between the mirrors —make the "V" wider or narrower—and see how many images are formed.

3 Cut a piece of heavy cardboard to measure about 1" wider than the mirrors you are using, and just as long. Cover the cardboard with black construction paper and glue it in place. Or use black tempera paint to make one side of the cardboard black.

4 Now decide how big an angle — how wide a "V" — you want your kaleidoscope to have. (As you found in Step 2, you can vary the number of reflected images by changing the angle.) Make sure the shiny sides of the mirrors are *facing* each other, and tape two long sides of your mirrors together in the "V" shape you want.

5 Measure the widest distance across the opening between the two mirrors. Trim the width of the black cardboard so that it measures the same as the opening between the mirrors. Tape the cardboard to the mirrors with the black side facing *in*, forming a three-sided "tube." You may need a friend to help you hold the three pieces while you tape them. Wrap the tape around as shown in the diagram.

BLACK SIDE OF CARDBOARD FACES IN

6 Cover one open end of the tube with a clear triangle of plastic cut from a notebook divider or food-container lid. Secure it in place with fast-drying glue and tape—but don't let too much tape show on the plastic.

CLEAR PLASTIC FROM NOTEBOOK DIVIDER

GLUE

7 Measure and cut three pieces of heavy cardboard, each one ¼" wider and longer than the

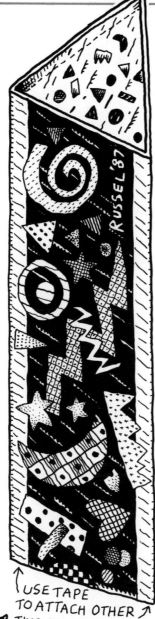

RUSSEL '87

↑ USE TAPE TO ATTACH OTHER ↑ TWO CARDBOARD COVERS

triangular tube. These will be the covering for your kaleidoscope. Attach them to the outside of the tube so that they stick out ¼" beyond the plastic-covered end of the tube. **Important:** Don't put glue on the backs of your mirrors. You can glue one cardboard cover to the black cardboard side of the tube, and then *use tape* to attach the other two cardboard covers.

8 Cut some pieces of unwanted color film slides or transparent colored plastic into small

PIECES OF COLORED PLASTIC OR FILM

shapes. You can also use confetti. Stand your kaleidoscope on end, with the clear plastic window facing up. Put about a dozen of these pieces on top of the clear window.

9 Find a "frosted" lid from a food container —one that lets light through, but that you can't see through completely. Cut a triangle of this plastic just big enough to cover the end of the tube. With the confetti and colored bits still in place on the clear window, place the frosted window on top of them. Glue or tape it in place. The confetti is now sandwiched between the frosted window and the clear window.

GLUE "FROSTED" TRIANGLE FROM FOOD CONTAINER LID

10 Finally, cut a triangle of heavy cardboard big enough to cover the other end of the kaleidoscope, and make a peephole in it about as wide as a pencil and off-center — closer to one corner than the others. Glue and tape this triangle in place, with the peephole closest to point of the "V" made by the mirrors.

PUT PEEPHOLE CLOSEST TO "V" MADE BY MIRRORS

11 Aim your kaleidoscope at a light (*not* direct sunlight) and look through the peephole. What do you see? Turn your scope slowly as you look at the light. What are your chances of seeing the same pattern twice?

VARIATION

■ If you want to try the deluxe kaleidoscope model, use a third mirror instead of the black cardboard floor.

AFTERWORDS

Your kaleidoscope is similar to one designed and patented by a Scottish physicist, Sir David Brewster, in 1817. Brewster's invention was so popular he sold more than 200,000 of them in the first few months. Brewster also came up with an even more fascinating version: a kaleidoscope with a convex lens mounted in the end instead of the plastic bits and confetti. Viewed through this device, the whole world becomes a series of symmetrical patterns, and even the plainest images look like blossoming flowers!

But kaleidoscopes can be more than toys. Until recently, a designer might use a kaleidoscope to create new patterns for such things as fabrics, carpets, and wallpaper. Now, however, designers more often use a computer to do the same job.

Your kaleidoscope also demonstrates some physical concepts, such as *opacity:* the ability of a substance to block out light. If you hold a piece of plywood between yourself and a burning candle, you won't see the candle *or* the light coming from the flame. That's because plywood is *opaque:* It doesn't let any light or sight through.

The opposite of opaque is *transparent.* Ordinary window glass is a good example of a transparent material. If you hold a piece of glass between you and the candle, you can *see* not only the light coming from the candle, but also the details of the candle's shape, size, color, and position. Transparent materials let light and sight through.

But what happens when you look at a burning candle through a sheet of waxed paper? You can *see some* light coming from the candle — certainly enough to tell whether or not the candle is lit. But you can't *see* any of the details. Waxed paper is a good example of a *translucent* material: It lets through some light, but not sight. How many other examples of translucent substances can you name? How would you describe the opacity of a glass of milk? The glass just after you finish drinking the milk?

Another principle at work in your kaleidoscope involves the *reflection* of light. First of all, light tends to travel in straight lines. Light entering a mirror in a straight line will reflect off the mirror in a straight line. But if the light hits the mirror at an angle, it will bounce off the mirror in the *opposite* direction, but at the same angle. This is the law of reflection: The angle going in has to equal the angle coming out. You can test this law by standing in front of a mirror that is only *half* as tall as you are. Surprisingly, you will be able to see your *whole* body, even though the mirror does not seem to be tall enough to do that job.

Most kaleidoscopes use about a 60-degree angle, which produces a six-sided pattern. Each side is an equal "slice" of the circle. The smaller the angle, the more images it creates. For instance, mirrors angled at 45 degrees will reflect eight equal images. You can figure out how many images you'll see with any given angle by measuring the angle with a compass and dividing the size of the angle into 360 — the number of degrees in a full circle. But as you probably noticed, *too* many repeated images can look too confusing. So cut down on the number of "slices" in your kaleidoscope pie!

KARATE CHOP VEGGIES

KARATE CHOP VEGGIES

Hiiiiiiiiyaa! Karate-chop your veggies and watch them grow. You don't have to be a karate expert or own a samurai sword. All you need is 15 minutes to set up this experiment—and earn a Black Belt in indoor gardening!

YOU WILL NEED

Several root vegetables such as carrots, beets, turnips, parsnips, radishes, and rutabagas
Knife
Pebbles or gravel
Several shallow bowls
1 Very large carrot
Heavy string or twine
2 Sweet potatoes
2 Empty jars or large glasses
Toothpicks

Is there food in the roots of a plant? There must be, because carrots, radishes, and beets are all roots that we eat. They have sugar and starch in them. If people can use that food as fuel or energy, then maybe the plants can use it too. Find out how much energy is available by growing Karate Chop Veggies this month.

1 Look at several root vegetables, such as carrots, beets, turnips, parsnips, and radishes. Which side do you think is "up" when they are in the ground? Which is the top? Figure out where the leaves come out on each vegetable. That is the growing tip. If there are leaves already growing on the veggies, remove them without cutting into the growing tip. With a knife (you might ask an adult to help you), chop off the bottoms of the root vegetables, leaving only about 1" or 2" of vegetable below the growing tip. (Save the vegetable bottoms to use in the Root-a-Bake recipe shown below.)

2 Choose several shallow bowls to grow your Karate Chop Veggies in. Put a layer of pebbles or gravel in each bowl. Set one vegetable top in each bowl, pushing the cut end down into the gravel to anchor it. Keep each bowl filled with ½" of water. New leaves should grow out of the top.

3 Will leaves grow upside down? Find out by making a hanging carrot basket. Use a very large, fat carrot. Cut off the bottom half, leaving about 5" of the fattest part, including the top. Hold the carrot cut-side up and hollow out a section big enough to hold some water. The widest part of the carrot—the growing tip—will be on the bottom. Make a rope hanger for the carrot using two pieces of twine or heavy string. Tie the strings together in the middle and then pull them up around the carrot, as shown. Hang the carrot basket from a hook or a bent coat hanger, near a window. Fill hollowed-out section with water. The leaves should sprout out of the bottom. But will they grow *down*?

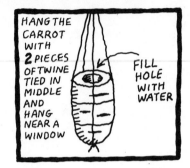

HANG THE CARROT WITH 2 PIECES OF TWINE TIED IN MIDDLE AND HANG NEAR A WINDOW

FILL HOLE WITH WATER

4 Which end is "up" on a sweet potato? Where will the leaves grow from? Look at two sweet potatoes. One end is more round than the other. One end has more of "scab" or scar than the other. Plant each sweet potato in a jar or glass of water to find out which end is the root. Plant one with the round end down. Plant the other with the round end up. Stick three toothpicks into the sides of the sweet potato as "arms" to support it in the glass. Keep the bottom third of the sweet potato covered with water. Set both jars in a warm, dark place until roots are formed. Then give the plants a little light, gradually. After a few days, you can place the sweet potatoes near a window for full light. When the sweet potato has sprouted many leaves, you can transfer it to a pot or the garden.

VARIATIONS

■ Chop off the top of a pineapple and grow it in pebbles or soil. If you use only pebbles and water, the leaves will continue to grow for a week or more. In soil, you can start a whole new plant.

■ Cut a potato into several pieces. Make sure that each piece has an "eye." Plant each piece in a separate pot of soil or in the garden.

ROOT-A-BAKE

2 Large carrots
2 Large parsnips
1 Large turnip
3 Tablespoons butter
¼ Cup brown sugar
Salt and pepper

CARROT

PARSNIP

TURNIP

RADISH

BUTTER

BEET

Preheat oven to 350°. Use the vegetables above or use the leftover bottom parts of your Karate Chop Veggies; any combination of root vegetables will do. Cut the vegetables into sticks about 3" by ½". Cook 10 minutes, or until tender, in boiling water. Drain. Butter a small, shallow baking dish and arrange the vegetables in it. Sprinkle brown sugar over them and dot with more butter. Add salt and pepper to taste. Bake at 350° for 20 to 25 minutes, until the brown sugar and butter form a glaze.

AFTERWORDS

Have you ever seen a carrot flower? Probably not, and neither have most of the farmers who grow acres and acres of carrots each year. But carrots *do* have flowers and they do bear fruit. The problem is: They are *biennial* plants, which means that it takes them two years to complete their growing cycle. They don't flower until the second year. And since carrots are grown mainly for the edible root, they are pulled up out of the ground after just one growing season, before the flower ever has a chance to develop.

Turnips, rutabagas, parsnips, and beets are also biennial plants. But in most cases, these vegetables too are harvested after only a few months of growth. Usually these plants are grown for their roots, which store up large amounts of starch and sometimes sugar. The leaves of the young plants are small, and the stems are short. If harvested early, these plants become food for people. But if they are allowed to remain in the ground for another year, all of the food stored in these plants is then put to use by the plants themselves, and the stored starch is used to produce more leaves on a taller stem. In your Karate Chop activity, you coaxed the vegetables into using up the food stored in the root to produce more leaves. If the carrot had remained in the ground, it would have produced more leaves and even a flower or two.

Most root vegetables are grown just for the root, but turnips are an exception. In the South, many people eat the turnip greens—the leaves from the top of the plant—and throw the root away! In other parts of the country, people eat the root and throw the turnip tops away!

Red beets are grown for the root, but another beet is grown mostly for its green top, called Swiss chard. A third kind of beet is one that you probably eat almost every day. You sprinkle this root on your cereal. You bake cookies and cakes with this root. Can you guess what it is? It's the sugar beet, from which much of the world's sugar is made. In fact, the sugar in sugar beets is identical to the sugar in sugar cane. Both form a crystalline sugar when the juice is extracted from the plant.

Is a white potato a root? No, although sweet potatoes are. White potatoes are called *tubers* and they are actually underground stems. Each "eye" on the potato is like a bud on a twig. That's why farmers are able to cut up potatoes into several small pieces and plant the pieces to start new potato plants. As long as each piece has an eye, or bud, the potato will grow new leaves and more tubers.

Although quite a few roots are edible, most plants do not store food in their roots. In most plants, the roots are mainly an anchor for the plant and a system for carrying water and minerals to the stem. And the bigger the plant, the bigger the root system must be. Some trees have lateral root systems, spreading out horizontally, that are almost twice as wide as the tree is tall. A 37-foot-tall oak might have roots reaching out 60 feet from the base of the tree! A good rule of thumb is that the roots usually extend farther than the branches do. So next time you're standing under a large tree, look at the spread of the branches. Then walk just until you are no longer under the tree. More likely than not, there are roots under your feet!

SHOO FLY, FRUIT FLY

SHOO FLY, FRUIT FLY

Don't say "Shoo, fly!" to fruit flies. They may be pesty, but scientists love to study them and so will you. You can raise two whole generations of fruit flies in a month (but it's best to try it in a *summer* month). It will take you 15 minutes to set up a habitat for them, and 30 minutes to observe them up close.

YOU WILL NEED

3 Large empty glass jars
Very ripe grapes and
    bananas
Paper towels
Absorbent cotton (large
    pieces, not cotton balls)
Sheet of notebook paper
Transparent tape
Very small clear glass or
    plastic bottle, such as an
    aspirin bottle
Aluminum foil
Magnifying glass

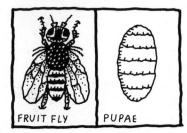

FRUIT FLY   PUPAE

Have you ever seen a bowl of fruit with fruit flies hovering around it? Did you wonder where the fruit flies came from? And why do they always seem to appear out of nowhere when fruit gets very ripe? It's easy to find out the answers by setting up a scientific experiment with two jars of fruit—one jar sealed up, the other jar open. Maybe the fruit flies are attracted to the ripe fruit. Or maybe the fruit-fly eggs are *on the fruit itself*—just waiting to hatch. Which is it?

1 Place half of a very ripe banana—with the peel still on—in a large, clean glass jar. Add some very ripe grapes and a crumpled paper towel. Close the mouth of the jar with loosely packed absorbent cotton, as shown. Make sure there are no holes around the edges, so that fruit flies can't get in or out.

2 Use a sheet of notebook paper and transparent tape to make a paper funnel that will fit in the mouth of the second jar. Let the small opening of the funnel be about ½" wide. Put some very ripe grapes and the other half of the banana in another jar, along with a crumpled paper towel. Set the paper funnel in the mouth of the jar. This forms a sort of trap, so that fruit flies can get *into* the jar but won't find their way *out* so easily.

3 Set both jars in a warm, bright spot, but not in direct sunlight. Within a few days, you should see some fruit flies. Are there fruit flies in both jars? Where did they come from? When you see 5 to 8 fruit flies in the jar with the funnel, remove the funnel and plug the mouth of the jar with absorbent cotton so they can't get out.

4 Watch the life cycle of the fruit flies in your jars. The eggs will be too tiny to see. But you can watch for the *larvae*—the crawling, worm-like stage in the development of the fruit fly. You might see them on the crumpled paper towel. They will eat the fruit for about a week and then change into the *pupae* stage. The pupae are almost adults, but not quite. When the pupae become adults, they will mate and then lay eggs. A few days after that, you will see new larvae, and the cycle will start all over again. Fruit flies live about four weeks all together. Count the fruit flies in your jar and see how fast they multiply.

5 Carefully transfer one or two of the new fruit flies to a very small empty jar, like an aspirin bottle. Wrap aluminum foil around the top two-thirds of the bottle, to make it dark inside. The fruit flies will move toward the light at the uncovered end of the bottle. Use a magnifying glass to observe them. Females are larger than the males. But

males have a larger, darker black band on the end on their abdomens. Can you tell which is which? If you think you have a male and female in your small bottle, transfer these fruit flies to the third large glass jar and add some fruit. Plug the opening with absorbent cotton. If you were right, these two fruit flies will mate and lay eggs. You can raise a whole new generation of fruit flies this way.

VARIATIONS

■ Place fruit in a jar but *do not* cover it at all. You may want to place the jar outdoors. Do fruit flies hover around the fruit? For how many days? Will they lay eggs and start a new generation? Does the fruit-fly population increase?

■ Try to raise fruit flies using different kinds of fruit. Find out whether or not you will get fruit flies with an apple, a pear, some cherries, or a peach.

AFTERWORDS

No matter how annoying it is to see a swarm of fruit flies circling around a beautiful bowl of fruit, scientists have often been willing to put up with the little buggers because fruit flies are perfect for one thing: the study of *genetics*. Genetics is the study of genes, and how different characteristics are passed along from parents to off-spring. With fruit flies, which live for only about four weeks, a geneticist can follow 25 generations of fruit flies in a year! Fruit flies are also easy for scientists to obtain. Since fruit flies thrive in a warm environment—such as overripe fruit —scientists have a constant supply.

The fruit flies you raised are called *Drosophila*—the same species used in the study of genes. Imagine that you had a male fruit fly with curly wings and a female fruit fly with normal wings. Will their children have curly or normal wings? It only takes four weeks to find out, because the whole life cycle of the fruit fly is complete in that amount of time.

Drosophila have very large chromosomes— although all chromosomes are microscopic—which

makes them easy to study. When the genes for several different traits are located together on one chromosome, scientists say that those genes are *linked*. So what happens if the gene for curly wings is linked to the male sex gene? In that case, only the male offspring of the fruit fly will have curly wings. Scientists have found that the fruit fly has more than 400 different genes, many of them linked together, so that there are a great number of variations in the ways fruit flies develop.

Can you see the color of your fruit flies' eyes? Believe it or not, they come in red, purple, white, apricot, and brown—not to mention the "bar-eyed" fruit flies and the ones with no eyes at all! Some of these colors are *dominant*, meaning that if only one parent passes that gene along to the child, the child will have the dominant trait. Other eye colors are *recessive* traits, meaning that *both* parents must pass the gene along in order for the child to have that trait. The same is true in human beings. Some eye colors are dominant— brown, for instance. Other eye colors, such as blue, are

recessive.

Surprisingly, some genes for eye color in fruit flies are linked to the gene that determines life expectancy. How long will a purple-eyed fruit fly live? Only about 27 days. Fruit flies with normal eyes will live about 10 days longer.

Of course, fruit flies *are* pests, and they've done enormous amounts of damage as well. The Mediterranean fruit fly took hold in Florida in the 1920s, threatening to destroy acres upon acres of fruit. Eliminating the Mediterranean fruit fly cost $6 million and the effort lasted for several years—only to have the "Med fly" pop up in California again in the 1970s.

Another damaging species is the Mexican fruit fly, which attacks citrus fruits. Then there's the apple maggot, the cherry fruit fly, the melon fly, and others that attack walnuts, celery, asparagus, and olives. And it's very hard to get rid of them.

Luckily for you, it's pretty easy to get rid of *your* fruit flies. Just dump the project in the trash, seal it—and keep your fruit in the refrigerator from now on!

GREASY KID STUFF

GREASY KID STUFF

Even if you don't like steak, french fries, or butter, you may be living off the fat of the land. Find out which foods are high in fat content by doing two easy kitchen experiments. You'll burn 110 calories of fuel or fat in the one hour it takes to complete this activity.

YOU WILL NEED

Brown paper bag
Various test foods such as:
    butter, banana, apple, hard-boiled egg, uncooked frankfurter, potato, avocado, tomato, cottage cheese, cookies, nuts, cola, orange, lima beans, peanut butter, potato chips, etc.
Pen or felt marker

Have you heard all about the four food groups and their role in planning a healthy, well-balanced diet? If so, you know that you should eat Fruits and Vegetables, Milk and Dairy Foods, Meats/Fish/Poultry/Dried Beans, and Breads and Cereals every day. But there's another rule about nutrition that is just as impor-

tant for good health, and that is the rule about fats in your diet. Health experts suggest that no more than 30% to 35% of the calories you eat should come from fats.

But before you can plan a healthy, low-fat meal, you need to find out which foods are high in fats, and which foods are not. Greasy Kid Stuff will help you sort out the "fat" foods from the other ones!

DEFINITIONS

Calorie: This is a unit of measure that refers to the amount of heat or energy a food will produce. Different foods will produce different amounts of energy. Ounce for ounce, fats will produce a lot more heat or energy than proteins or carbohydrates, and so fats are high in calories.

Carbohydrates: Almost all carbohydrates come from plants. There are two main kinds of foods in the carbo-hydrates group — sugars and starches. Peaches and berries are sugary carbohydrates, while peas and potatoes are starchy carbohydrates. Wheat,

rice, and the other grains are primarily starch as well.

Protein: Every living cell contains protein, which is why meats, fish, and poultry are such good sources of this important kind of food. Milk and dairy products are also very rich in protein, and so are dried peas and beans. Protein's main job is to help the body grow.

Fats: The oily or greasy part of meat, poultry, fish, nuts, seeds, and so on.

1 Cut open a large brown paper bag and lay it flat. This will be your Fats Chart. Cut off a small pat of butter and rub it on at the top of the paper-bag chart, until the butter stains. Write the word "Butter" under the stain, and put a number 10 beside it. Butter will make the greasiest stain, since it is almost *all* fat.

2 Next, look at all of the foods you're going to test, and try to decide which one has the *least* fat in it. Rub that food on the bag

near the bottom. Write the name of the food underneath the stain it makes, and put a number 1 beside it.

3 Now try to decide where the other test foods fit in the scale from 1 to 10. If you think peaches are very fatty, put them near the top of the chart and give them a high number. Continue testing foods for fat by rubbing each food on the bag and numbering the stains. With dry foods like cookies, you may want to warm them in your hands first, and then rub hard to make a mark. Label each stain by writing the name of the food underneath it.

4 Look at the bag a few hours later — or the next day — when the wet stains have dried. Hold the bag up to the light and you will see a greasy, see-through mark by each food that con-tains fat. The more fat in the food, the greasier the stain will be. Did you put all of the foods in the right order? If so, you will have a column of stains that goes from very greasy to not greasy at all. If you find a big greasy mark near the bottom of your scale, or a "blank" space near the top, you guessed wrong about the fat content of the foods!

Does the mark from the banana surprise you? How about the stain above the word cheese? Did you know that many nutritious foods are very high in fat?

HOW TO LOSE FAT—FAST!

When it comes to cooking hamburgers, there's a great way to cut your own fat in-take. It's called *broiling*. Find out how much fat you can lose—from a hamburger patty, that is—by trying this dinner-time experiment.

■ Divide a pound of ground beef into four hamburger patties, each weighing about ¼ pound. Try to make the patties as equal in size as possible.

■ Fry two of the hamburgers in a skillet on top of the stove.

Broil two of them in a broiler pan in the oven.

■ When the hamburgers are cooked, look in the pans to see how much fat they've lost. Which cooking method removed the most fat from the hamburgers? Measure the fat in the broiler by scooping it out a tablespoon at a time.

Then do the same with the fat in the frying pan—if there is any! If there *isn't* any fat in the frying pan, where is it?

■ Did you know that most butcher shops and meat departments add chunks of white fat to the beef before grinding it into hamburger? By law, hamburger may contain

61

as much as 30% added fat. That's in addition to the fat that is already present in the red part of the meat!

VARIATIONS

■ Go on a Supermarket Safari looking for fats! Read the ingredients labels on cookies, crackers, cakes, frozen doughnuts, breakfast cereals, etc. You'll be surprised how many dessert foods contain beef fat or other animal fats. Next, read and compare the nutrition information labels on many different foods. Make a chart showing how many grams of fat there are in a single serving of whole milk, low-fat milk, cottage cheese, one pat of butter, various canned soups, frozen dinners, potato chips, breads, and so on.

■ Which foods are most satisfying? Eat a meal that is entirely fat-free. You may want to consult your brown bag chart of grease stains and your Supermarket Safari list to help you decide what your fat-free meal should have in it. After your fat-free meal, how long is it until you are hungry again? The next day, eat a starch-free meal and make a note of when your hunger pangs return.

AFTERWORDS

Fats have fallen into disfavor recently, especially among people who are concerned about heart disease and good health. Nevertheless, fats are a necessary and important part of any diet. For one thing, fats provide a good source of energy. They also slow down the rate of digestion, which means that you will feel "satisfied" longer after eating a high-fat meal. Fats carry the fat-soluble vitamins A, D, E, and K; these vitamins can be dissolved only in fat and not in water like the other vitamins. And lastly, many fats contain an essential nutrient, linoleic acid, that is necessary for normal growth and healthy skin.

The problem is that most Americans eat *too many* fats. Since the early 1900s, American consumption of fat has risen 25%, while consumption of carbohydrates has fallen by the same amount. This trend is probably an unhealthy one, because there seems to be a connection between the amount of saturated fat you eat and your chance of getting heart disease and certain kinds of cancer. For this reason, many nutrition experts recommend that fats account for no

more than 30% to 35% of the calories consumed daily. The average American diet, however, currently contains about 45% fat.

In any plan to reduce fats in your diet, the key word is *saturated*. Saturated fats are thought to contain larger amounts of cholesterol than polyunsaturated fats. And although the question of cholesterol levels is still being debated, many doctors suggest that people with a history of high blood pressure and/or heart disease should cut down on high-cholesterol foods.

But how do you know which fats are saturated and which fats are not? Here are some easy guidelines to help you answer that question. Saturated fats are usually solid at room temperature, and they come primarily from animal sources—meat, milk and dairy products, and eggs. *Polyunsaturated* fats, on the other hand, are usually liquid at room temperature. They come from vegetable sources—safflower oil and corn oil are two examples—and they are thought to help *decrease*

the level of cholesterol in the blood. The two *monounsaturated* fats, olive oil and peanut oil, also have a positive effect on cholesterol levels.

For people who want to cut down on cholesterol, it's animal fats that must be eliminated. This can mean switching from butter to margarine, cutting down on the number of eggs eaten each week, choosing skim milk instead of whole milk at mealtimes, and eating leaner cuts of meat.

But in any discussion of nutrition it's important to remember that no single nutrient should be completely eliminated from the diet. Cholesterol is a good example of this rule. In fact, cholesterol is needed by the body for digestion and for the formation of hormones and vitamin D. Your body can probably manufacture all the cholesterol you need. But it would still be a mistake to cut out all foods that contain cholesterol, because many of those foods provide *other* valuable nutrients that are of great importance in a well-balanced diet.

ROCKETS AWAY

ROCKETS AWAY

Do you have dreams of being an astronaut? First you have to learn how to get your rocketship off the ground. You'll be airborne in only 30 minutes!

YOU WILL NEED

A plastic tennis-ball can or plastic soda bottle with cap
Large nail or pencil
Scissors
Soda straws of 3 different types: jumbo, super jumbo, and flexible (see **Note**)
Tape
Paper
Several small pieces of hook Velcro
A "woolly" blanket
A plastic bag, about 10" by 12"
Some fishing line, 6- or 8-pound test
A few balloons, *long* rather than round
Vinegar
Baking soda

Note: Most large drinking straws—the kind you get at burger joints—are *jumbo* straws. However, a few fast-food places (like Burger King or ice-cream parlors that serve thick milk shakes) have even larger straws—*super jumbo*. For this activity you will need a few of each and the jumbo should be able to pass smoothly *through* the super jumbo. You might also want to get some *flexible* straws (ones that have a bend like an accordion partway down the straw); they're available at the supermarket.

You can use air power to learn some rules that are important for understanding flight and trajectory (the path your rocketship will take in space). Get set to make your own rockets and a launcher!

1 Poke a hole in the lid of the plastic tennis-ball can with a large nail or pencil. If using a soda bottle, you might have to use a drill to make a hole in the cap. Or try using the pointed end of a pair of scissors. (Ask a grown-up for help if you need it.)

2 Cut the end of the flex straw on an angle and run it through the hole in the lid or cap. The straw should fit very snug. Put the lid or cap back on the can or bottle.

3 Stick a *jumbo* straw into the end of the flex straw and tape it in place. The flex straw will allow you to adjust the angle of launch during later experiments. Your rocket launcher is now complete!

POKE HOLE IN LID
CUT ANGLE
TAPE JUMBO TO FLEXIBLE STRAW
PLASTIC TENNIS BALL CAN

4 Now, make some rockets. Fold over ½" of the end of a *super jumbo* straw and tape it down. Slide the super jumbo over the jumbo launcher straw, aim, and give the can or bottle a sharp squeeze. The super jumbo should take off! Practice launches to see if you can land your rocket in a box or wastebasket. Try it from different locations around the room. Then put some obstacles in its path to see if you can get your rocket high enough to sail over them.

VARIATIONS

■ *Stabilizers* are often attached to flying devices to help them fly straight. Find out how various stabilizer designs help or hinder the straight flight of your rockets. Tape on paper fins (2, 3, or 4), cones, or other designs.

■ Does a short rocket fly farther than a long one? Make different rockets (2", 4", and 6" long), fit them all with identical stabilizers, and find out which flies best.

■ A target makes all of the experiments more interesting! Get a bit of *hook Velcro* and tape it to the front tip of your rockets. Search around the house for a blanket that the

Velcro-tipped rocket will easily stick to. Hang the blanket over a door. Now launch the rocket and try to stick it to the blanket. How high can you stick a rocket? What is the greatest distance from which you can stick the rocket to the blanket?

■ Make a Beeline Rocket Message Delivery System. Tape the soda straw to the side seam of a plastic bag. Run a length of fishing line through the straw long enough to tie one end of the line to something in one room, and the other end of the line to something in another room. Write a message and put it in the bag. The open end of the

ZOOM!

GIVE PLASTIC CAN A SHARP SQUEEZE!

PUT BALLOON INTO BAG WITH MESSAGE

TAPE SODA STRAW TO PLASTIC BAG

FISHING LINE

TAPE A BIT OF HOOK VELCRO TO END OF ROCKET

HANG BLANKET OVER DOOR OR TALL CHAIR

STRAWS

bag should face *away* from where you want your message to go. Blow up a balloon and pinch the opening shut, put it into the bag with the message, and release it. Your message will rocket into the next room!

■ Real rockets don't run on air, of course. They use fuel that burns, or *combusts,* and the power sends them off into space. You can make your own rocket fuel. Pour 1 cup of vinegar into the can or bottle. Then take 2 tablespoons of baking soda, roll it up into a paper napkin, and insert it in the can or bottle. Replace the lid or cap and swirl the container to mix the ingredients together. Zoom!

AFTERWORDS

Real rockets don't fly on compressed air power. Real rockets have *internal combustion engines* and carry both fuel to burn and a source of oxygen to help the combustion. Because rockets carry their own oxygen source, they can operate even in the deep reaches of space where very little air exists.

Rocket propulsion works because of a very basic law of physics: For every action, there is an equal, and opposite, reaction. Fuel is burned in a closed chamber. The hot gases that result from the combustion rush out the nozzle at great speed. The fast-moving gases that are propelled out the end of the rocket are the "action." The opposite "reaction" moves the rocket forward. This simple principle drives rockets to the moon and beyond!

Your soda-straw rocket carries no fuel for propulsion; the driving force behind the rocket is air pressure. When you squeeze the flexible plastic bottle, the air in the bottle is compressed into a smaller space and the pressure inside increases. The air pushes out in all directions with equal force. When the increased force pushes against the closed end of the rocket straw, the force is strong enough to send the rocket off into space.

If the force is applied for a short time, the rocket will move slower. The longer the force acts on the rocket, the faster the rocket will be going when it leaves the launcher.

This fact suggests that a longer straw rocket will fly faster (therefore farther) than a short one. Did you figure that out yourself?

For a brief moment during the launch of a soda-straw rocket, it acts like a real rocket. Precisely when the rocket leaves the launcher and the pressure inside the straw is vented through the open end of the straw, it acts just like a full-fledged rocket. For a split second, air will rush out the open end of the straw as it leaves the launcher. This action will have the *re*action of adding a little thrust to the straw rocket. The effect will be small, but nonetheless the thrust will help the rocket move. The rest of the rocket's flight can be attributed to the push given to the rocket by the action of compressed air.

Another force to be dealt with in rocketry is air. Air is like a fluid; it has mass and occupies space. It must be pushed out of the way if an object is to pass through it. Therefore, the more streamlined you make your rocket, the more easily it will push through the air. Put this force to work *for* you. In order to keep the rocket on course, place stabilizers, or fins, at the back of the rocket. As long as the rocket travels straight forward, the sharp edges of the fins cut efficiently through the air and keep the rocket steady. But if the rocket starts to pitch or roll, the broad side of the fin will start to make contact with the air, creating more air *resistance.* Increased resistance will tend to slow down that side of the rocket, which corrects the rocket's flight automatically. Now your rockets should make it safely to their destinations!

MARBLEIZED PAPER

MARBLEIZED PAPER

How would you like to make wrapping paper that looks like real marble, with swirls of color? You don't have to be a great artist. Just put science to work for you and in about 30 minutes you can create a work of art.

YOU WILL NEED

3 Drinking glasses
Water
Small amounts of assorted beverages (milk, juices, soft drinks) and household liquids (vinegar, detergents)
Teaspoon
Salt
Vegetable oil
Food coloring
Newspapers
A large rectangular baking dish, tray, dishpan, or disposable aluminum roasting pan, big enough to hold the paper
Hobby paints: *oil-based*, in various colors (available in small square jars wherever model airplanes are sold)
Stick or paint stirrer
White notepaper and sheets of paper large enough to be used as gift wrap (pads of artist's "layout bond" work well)
Dishwashing liquid
Salad oil or turpentine or paint thinner for clean-up
Paper towels

Maybe you've heard that oil and water don't mix. But are there other liquids that won't mix with water? Is there a way to *force* oil and water to mix? When you find out the answers to those questions, you'll understand why marbleized paper is easy to make.

1 Fill a drinking glass half full of water and add a small amount of milk. Stir. Do the two liquids mix together or do they separate? Rinse out the glass and try the experiment with other beverages. Do all liquids mix with water? Can you find a liquid in your kitchen that will *not* mix with water? **CAUTION:** DO NOT DRINK THE EXPERIMENTS!

2 Clean the glasses and begin again. Fill one glass with cold water and one glass with hot water. At the same time, add a teaspoon of salt to each glass and stir. Which glass of water dissolves the salt faster? Pour ½ cup of vegetable oil into the third glass, add a teaspoon of salt, and stir. What happens?

3 Find out whether or not you can *make* oil and water mix! Start with a clean glass, filled halfway with water. Add a few drops of food coloring, so you'll be able to tell the water from the oil more easily. Now add a few teaspoonfuls of vegetable oil and stir madly! If you stir fast enough, will the oil and water finally mix? Does the food coloring mix better with the oil or water?

4 Now it's time to take advantage of the Great Oil and Water Feud and make beautiful marbleized paper! Spread newspapers on the floor near your workspace to use as a drying area. Fill your flat baking dish, tray, or disposable roasting pan half full of water. Add a small amount of hobby paint to the water. See how it floats on the surface? Use a stick to swirl

HOBBY PAINT WILL FLOAT ON SURFACE

the paint around. You can marbleize your paper now, or add more colors first. When the floating paints look good to you, lay the paper on the surface of the water for a few seconds. (Until you get the hang of it, experiment with the small notepaper before you go on to the larger paper.) Work quickly and don't soak the paper. That way it won't wrinkle. Lift it off and look at your designs! You'll probably be able to marbleize one or two more sheets of paper before you need to add more paint. Experiment with stirring

the water rapidly and then quickly putting the paper on the surface while the paint and water are still moving.

5 Find our how soap affects the oil-and-water combination by adding a squirt of dishwashing liquid to the mixture. What happens if you add the soap without stirring the paint and water? What happens if you stir it up first? Can you get different marbleized effects this way?

6 Let your marbleized paper dry, paint-side up, on newspapers for several hours before using it. If the paper is slightly wrinkled, you can iron it between two sheets of plain paper. Use a low setting on your iron.

7 Clean your marbleizing tray and utensils with salad oil or paint thinner.

VARIATIONS

■ You can marbleize vases, cardboard and plastic boxes, pencils, and other objects that have a smooth, solid-color surface. Boxes can be marbleized in the tray by simply laying the box on the surface of the water, one side at a time. For other objects, use a bucket of water instead of a tray, and

get the water moving before you dip the object.

■ Create special designs by swirling a marbleizing "comb" through the floating paints. You can make the comb yourself: Use a strip of heavy cardboard about 1" wide and 8" long; push some pins through the cardboard in a straight row, spaced ½ inch apart. Or use toothpicks stuck into a piece of Styrofoam.

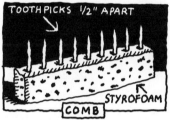
TOOTHPICKS ½" APART
COMB STYROFOAM

■ To make marbleized note cards and envelopes, use sheets of stationery folded in half. If you dip the envelopes, don't use too much paint and be sure to keep the gummed flaps *dry.* You can write on your marbleized paper if the paint isn't too thick.

■ Make book covers from your marbleized paper. Or better yet, "publish" your own book and paste the marbleized paper on the inside of the front and back covers. That's the way it's done for special editions of handmade books.

AFTERWORDS

Marbleized paper was created in Persia 400 years ago, and it has been made just about the same way ever since. In France, England, Italy, and, later, in the United States, beautiful marbleized papers were often used as endpapers: the decorative papers that are pasted down on the *inside* front and back covers of books. For an example, you might check your local public library and/or school library. If they have old copies of Webster's New International Dictionary, Second Edition, the endpapers will probably be marbleized paper.

Other old books in your library might have a variation of marbleized paper: marbled edges. Even as recently as the 1950s, apprentice bookbinders were taught how to marbleize book edges by hand. The pages of the book were held tightly together in a clamp, and then dipped quickly into the multicolored paints floating on the surface in a vat of water. Master bookbinders knew how to use combs and rakes to create specific standard patterns with names like Peacock and Agate.

Today marbleized endpapers and edges are rarely used, but when they do appear, they are still made by hand, and still use the principle that oil and water won't mix. But water mixes well with most other substances. In fact, water can dissolve so many substances that chemists call it a *universal solvent.* The substance a solvent dissolves is called the *solute,* and the mixture that results is called a *solution.*

Your kitchen is full of solutions that you drink every day. Lemonade, coffee, tea, apple juice, and soft drinks are all solutions with one or more solutes dissolved in them. Have you ever noticed that sugar dissolves more easily in hot tea than in iced tea? That's because the *solubility* of a solid — in other words, the ability of a solid to dissolve — increases when the temperature of the solvent goes up.

But here's a surprise: The opposite is true when the solute is a *gas.* With gases, the colder the solvent, the more soluble the gas is. Maybe you didn't even know that gases could be dissolved! Well, they can — and that's how soft drinks are made. The gas *carbon dioxide* is actually dissolved in water, along with sugar and some other flavors, to make the fizzy carbonated drinks people love. Now that you know how temperature affects the solubility of gases, you can understand why sodas left out in warm weather always taste flat!

One beverage you'll find in your refrigerator isn't a solution at all. Scientists call milk a *colloid,* rather than a solution, because there is something in milk that can't be dissolved. Can you guess what it is? It's the butterfat, of course! Fifty years ago, before milk was homogenized, the cream — which has most of the butterfat — would separate from the milk and rise to the top of the bottle. (That was in the days when milk came in bottles.) Though cream looks thicker and "heavier" than milk, the tiny particles of fat in cream are lighter than the rest of the milk.

Today, however, the butterfat never separates from the milk because homogenization is standard in the United States. During this milk-processing method, the small particles of butterfat are forced through a valve and made even smaller. Once the butterfat particles are the right size, they neither rise nor sink, because they aren't lighter or heavier than the rest of the milk.

So next time you sip a glass of milk, you can say thanks to technology for the homogenization that gives you a smoother drink. But when it comes to making marbleized paper, there is no need for technological tricks. The natural conflict between oil and water brings about a more beautiful creation.

ICE CREAM MACHINE

ICE CREAM MACHINE

Which is colder: ice or ice cream? You'll find out when you get the scoop on the amazing Ice-Cream Machine! From mixing to tasting should take about 45 minutes.

YOU WILL NEED

Empty coffee can with
  plastic lid
Scissors
Wooden spoon
Ingredients for Vanilla Cookie
  Ice Cream (see box)

Bowl
Electric mixer
5-Pound bag of ice
Brown grocery bag
Hammer
Newspapers
Bucket

2 to 2½ Cups table salt
Empty plastic container or
  ice-cube tray

Homemade ice cream and clear roads during a winter blizzard—what do these two things have in common? They

both depend on the special relationship between ice and salt. Salt melts ice: That's why it's spread on icy roads in the winter. But salt also causes the temperature of water to go down. You'll use salt to melt ice and lower the temperature of the water in your Ice-Cream Machine. Believe it or not, the water will get colder than 32 degrees Fahrenheit—but it won't freeze! Pretty cool, huh?

INGREDIENTS FOR VANILLA COOKIE ICE CREAM

(adapted from a recipe published in *Consumer Reports* magazine)

1 Egg
⅔ Cup sugar
1 Teaspoon vanilla
1 Cup heavy cream
2 Cups half-and-half
¾ Cup of your favorite cookies, crushed by hand

1 Before you begin, have ready all the ingredients for Vanilla Cookie Ice Cream and all of the equipment listed. Wash and dry the empty coffee can and lid. Using a scissors, poke a small hole in the plastic lid. Make sure the hole is *off-center*. Enlarge the hole by pushing the wooden-spoon handle through the hole. Don't make the hole *too* big: The spoon handle should fit tightly in the hole. With the scissors, trim away the rough edges of plastic around the hole.

2 Make the ice-cream mix by putting the egg, sugar, and vanilla into a bowl and beating with an electric mixer for 1 minute on a medium speed. Add the cream and half-and-half, and mix on low speed for 3 minutes. (You'll add the crushed cookies later.) Set the ice-cream mix back in the refrigerator until your bucket of ice is ready to go.

3 Now you need to make crushed ice. Put the 5-pound bag of ice inside a brown grocery bag, fold the bag end closed, and pound the ice with a hammer on the kitchen floor. It might help to cover the grocery bag with a layer of newspapers, to keep the hammer from breaking through the paper bag. Pour about one-third of the crushed ice into the bucket. Cover the ice with about ½ cup of salt. Put the coffee can on top of the ice, in the middle of the bucket. Add ice and salt in layers around the can until you have used up all of the ice. **But don't use all of the salt**

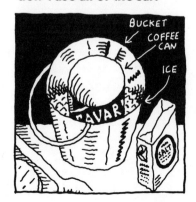

yet. You may not need it all, or you may need to add some later.

4 Pour about two-thirds of the ice-cream mix into the coffee can. Pour the rest of the mix into a plastic container or empty ice-cube tray and stick it in the freezer right away. This part of your ice-cream experiment is what scientists call the "control": It gives you another method of freezing your mixture so you can compare and see which method works best. When you have finished making ice cream, immediately check the control portion in the freezer. Is it frozen yet? Can you figure out why?

5 Stick the wooden spoon into the coffee can with the ice-cream mix. Snap on the plastic lid, letting the spoon handle stick up through the hole. The wooden spoon has two jobs in your ice-cream machine: It's a handle for turning the can, and a *dasher* for stirring the ice cream. Now grab this handle and start turning the can. Every 2 or 3 minutes, stop spinning the can and hold it still so you can use the dasher (the "bowl" of the wooden spoon) to stir the ingredients inside. Try to mix in as much air as you can: Move the dasher in a circular motion around the bottom of the can and the side. Don't remove the lid to do this.

After about 10 or 15 minutes of spinning the can, take the lid off and add the crushed cookies. Replace the lid and continue as before. You can check on your progress every once in a while, but don't take the lid off *too* often. You'll notice when you're stirring that the mixture is getting thicker. All together, it will probably take about 25 to 30 minutes to make ice cream. But don't worry: It's not hard work! You can keep the can spinning without much muscle power. And it never hurts to have a hungry friend handy, to help you take "turns"! **Remember:** When the ice cream is done, check the control portion in the freezer.

HINTS FOR SUCCESS:

- Make sure all the ice-cream ingredients are cold when you start.
- If the ice doesn't seem to be melting in the bottom of the bucket, add a small amount of water to get it going.
- Don't add too much salt at first: You can always add more later if you need it. The more salt you use, the faster the ice will melt. If the ice melts too fast, ice crystals will form and the mix will harden too soon —before you have a chance to stir enough air into it. Air is what gives ice cream its smooth texture. Air also keeps you from noticing how *cold* the ice cream is! Is your home-made ice cream colder than store-bought ice cream? Which do you think is the most "airy"?
- Be patient. At first, the ice cream may not seem to be solidifying, but after about 20 minutes, you'll notice the change.

AFTERWORDS

Ice cream is the delicious result of some important scientific principles. No one knows for sure when ice cream was invented, but frozen desserts have been around for a long time. The Romans had fruit ices, and Marco Polo claims to have eaten some ice milk during his travels to the Far East.

If you've eaten ice milk or fruit ices, however, you know that they just aren't…well, as *creamy* as ice cream. So who put the creaminess in ice cream? Probably the Europeans. In the 1700s they discovered that salt could lower the temperature of ice —and that meant that frozen desserts could be frozen much more quickly. When milk and cream are frozen quickly, ice crystals don't have time to form.

In your ice-cream experiment, you probably found out that it's hard to get the perfect balance between freezing the mixture quickly enough so that ice crystals can't form, and freezing it slowly enough so that you have time to incorporate plenty of air. "Overrun" is what ice-cream manufacturers call the air that is mixed into ice cream. Using huge machines with gigantic dashers, they can double the volume of ice cream by adding as much air as there is cream, sugar, and milk! Ice cream with a lot of overrun doesn't weigh very much, and it's pretty frothy in your mouth, too. But ice cream without air is too hard and too cold: It's more like frozen milk. The mixed-in air actually keeps you from noticing how cold the ice cream is!

To keep manufacturers from cheating the public by putting huge quantities of air into ice cream, the government requires that a gallon of ice cream weigh at least 4½ pounds. Next time you're in the grocery store, compare the less-expensive ice creams with the higher-priced ones. You can probably tell just by lifting them which ones are full of air. When you think about the fact that you're getting more *food* and less air in the heavier ice creams, doesn't it make the high price a little easier to swallow?

Modern-day manufacturers use huge freezers instead of salt and ice to freeze the ice cream ingredients. But before freezers were invented, people needed ice to make ice cream. Without refrigeration, though, it was hard to get ice in the summer. Some people, who lived near rivers or lakes, had icehouses to store ice in, and they could make ice cream in the summer. In winter, they took huge chunks of ice from the river and packed the giant ice cubes in hay for insulation. The ice lasted for months that way—but by August, it was often melted. In those days, ice cream was eaten more often in December than in the good old summertime. Quite a chilly treat!

People often wonder how salt can *melt* snow and ice on the roads if it actually makes ice water *colder*. And if the melted ice is colder than 32 degrees, then why doesn't it freeze again right away? The answer is that as the ice melts, it dissolves the salt and makes saltwater. Saltwater doesn't freeze at 32 degrees the way plain water does: It freezes at a *lower* temperature.

Now that you're an expert about ice cream, you might want to go into the ice-cream business. Maybe you'll be the first person to come up with a flavor no one's ever thought of yet. What a sweet life! Just try not to lick up all your profits!

SKYDIVER

SKYDIVER

What goes up must come down—but wearing a parachute makes landing easier! This activity will take 30 minutes, plus a few hours drying time for your papier-mâché paratrooper.

YOU WILL NEED

Small piece of cardboard
Scissors
Pipe cleaners
Flour
Water
Bowl and spoon
Newspapers
Tempera or hobby paints
Paintbrush
Plastic from garbage bags,
   dry-cleaning bags,
   or food-storage bags
Felt-tip marker
Needle
Heavy-duty thread

Did you know that even the most experienced paratroopers sometimes get hurt when parachuting out of an airplane? As the saying goes: "It's not the fall that hurts—it's the landing." Maybe you've wondered why these paratroopers hit the ground so hard.

It seems like there should be some way to keep them from falling so fast. Well, you'll find out why parachutes are designed the way they are when you make your own test pilot who's heading for a fall!

1 Cut out a body for your parachute man from a small piece of cardboard, using the pattern shown here. Your man should be about the same size as the pattern.

USE THIS FOR PATTERN AND PAINT YOUR OWN PARACHUTIST

2 Make a "loop" by twisting a pipe cleaner into the shape of a script *e*, as shown. (Later you'll tie your parachute to this loop.)

Place the loop against the cardboard man's neck so that the two tails of pipe cleaner stick out to form arms. Then wrap the arms around the neck once to attach the pipe cleaner to the man. This is the

MAKE SURE LOOP IS AWAY FROM BODY AND FREE TO TIE STRING TO IT.

frame for the parachute man.

3 Mix up some papier-mâché paste by combining 4 tablespoons flour with 6 tablespoons water in a small bowl. Cut or tear strips of newspaper about ½" wide. Dip a strip of newspaper into the paste and then use your fingers to wipe off the excess. Cover the arms, head, and body of the parachute man with strips of papier-mâché wrapping them around and around to

build up a little bulk. **But be sure to leave the loop free and uncovered!** Let the papier-mâché man dry for a few hours or overnight. Then you can paint a face and overalls on your parachutist.

FLO

BE SURE LOOP IS FREE

4 While the paint is drying, cut a circle out of lightweight plastic such as a garbage bag, food-storage bag, or the plastic that covers your clothes when they come back from the dry cleaner. This will be your parachute. How big a parachute will you need? Do you think a parachute could ever be *too* big? You'll find out by experimenting with circles of various sizes. If your man is less than 3" tall, you can start with a parachute 12" in diameter.

5 Now it's time to attach the lines to the parachute, and then to the man. First, look at your parachute circle and pretend it is a clock. With a felt-tip marker, put a dot each, about ¼" from the parachute edge, at 12 o'clock, 2 o'clock, 4 o'clock, 6 o'clock, 8 o'clock, and 10 o'clock. Thread a needle with a single strand of heavy-duty thread and attach six lines to the parachute, one at each dot, as shown in the diagram. How long should the lines be?

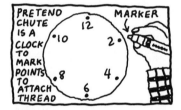

That depends on the size of your parachute. A good rule of thumb is to make the lines approximately as long as the parachute is wide. Once you have threaded the lines through the plastic, though, they will be double strands — half the width of the para-

chute. When all six lines are attached to the chute, pull them together and make sure that they are all *exactly* the same length. Knot them through the loop on the back of the parachute man's neck, as if they were all one thick cord.

6 Time to bail out! Experiment with your parachute man by tossing him into the air, or dropping him from the top of a ladder. But if you're going to climb a ladder, be sure to have an

adult nearby. You also can throw your parachute man out a window, but **never lean out the window!** Have a friend waiting below to watch where it lands.

When you drop him from a high place, does your para-

chute man fall gently to the ground or does he plummet to the earth? Does he swing from side to side as he descends? If so, cut a small hole — a little smaller than a dime — in the very center of the chute. This air vent helps stabilize the parachute's descent. Experiment with different-size chutes on the same man. Can you figure out why paratroopers don't want huge parachutes, even though bigger chutes would allow them to land more gently?

VARIATIONS

■ Attach the parachute man to a helium balloon and let it go. When the helium balloon gets high enough, it will explode, and the man will parachute to earth. This is how one of the first parachutists got the chance to test his new invention! If you write your name and address on the parachute in permanent marker before launching the balloon, you might get a letter or call from the person who finds it.

■ Before tying the lines (threads) to the man, arrange them so that one is shorter than the others. How does this affect the parachute man's fall?

AFTERWORDS

Imagine: Long before people had thought of a way to get themselves up off the ground, Leonardo da Vinci had devised a way to land safely: with a parachute. His drawing of a man descending in a square-framed parachute dates from around 1485 — a full 300 years before human beings first took to the skies in hot-air balloons! But in 1783, a Frenchman named Sebastien Lenormand actually built a parachute and tried it out himself by jumping from a tower in Paris. He survived, and is usually credited with having invented the parachute.

Ten years later, another Frenchman, André-Jacques Garnerin, constructed a parachute of white linen, 23 feet in diameter, and attached it to a hot-air balloon. Then he went up to 6,000 feet and cut the hot-air balloon free! As crowds of awestruck people watched silently from the ground, Garnerin came down. His descent was successful, but because his parachute had been designed without an air vent, he was swung violently from side to side. He fainted from the nauseating experience!

Parachutes wouldn't be necessary at all if it weren't for one thing: gravity. Gravity is the force that attracts two bodies to each other — any two bodies, although most of the time we are only aware of the Earth's gravity. Did you know that the force of gravity is present between everything — even between you and your lamp? It's just that it is very, very weak gravity — so weak that no matter how close you get to your lamp, it won't fall on you from the force of your own gravitational pull! Here's why: The mathematical equation that explains the force of gravity says basically that the force of gravity increases when the distance between the two bodies decreases. But it also says that the *mass* of the two bodies — how dense they are and how much they weigh — has a lot to do with how strong the gravitational force is. You and your lamp — or any other objects you get close to — don't weigh enough *together* to create a noticeable gravitational force.

Of course, there's gravity on the moon, too, but its force is not as powerful as the Earth's. That's why you weigh less on the moon than you do on Earth. Some people think that gravity is weaker on the moon because it's "way out in space." But that's not true. Gravity is weaker on the moon because the moon is smaller than Earth, and so it's gravitational pull on a human being is less. The moon would be a great place to practice parachuting. Even if your parachute didn't open, it wouldn't hurt half so much when you came down!

Stars, too, are subject to the laws of gravity, and they exert an enormous force on the smaller bodies around them. Take our sun, for instance, which is really a very near star. The sun has so much mass, it is able to attract the Earth and the other planets, and hold them in its power! If the sun were smaller and much less dense, the Earth would never have been pulled into orbit around the sun. It might have flown out into space and become a meteoroid instead. If the sun were larger and more dense, the Earth would be pulled right *to* the sun by the force of the sun's gravity, and burn up. Isn't it amazing that the sun's mass is just right to maintain its safe gravitational relationship with Earth?

SCIENCE MAGIC

SCIENCE MAGIC

Hocus pocus! It's time to focus on magic! You can learn to do all the tricks for this magic act in about 45 minutes. But it might take you longer to perform the best all-time disappearing trick—the one that makes your stage fright disappear!

YOU WILL NEED

Tray for props
5 Pennies
Plate
Raisins
Club soda
Several drinking glasses
Water
Handkerchief

ADVICE TO AMATEUR MAGICIANS

Some of the tricks you are about to learn have been used for many years by famous magicians. And yet they are very simple to do! But the first time you try these tricks, they may not seem totally amazing to your friends. Why not? For two reasons: One is that you need to practice them many times, so that you can do them smoothly and confidently. And the other thing you need, in order to really come off like a polished magician, is patter. Patter is all the small talk magicians make while they are performing the trick—or waiting for it to work! So be sure to use lots of snappy patter while performing your tricks. (But don't tell anyone we told you—because that's a trick of the trade!)

GOOD VIBRATIONS: A MIND-READING COIN TRICK

Have 4 or 5 pennies ready, each with a different date. *Make sure you don't handle the pennies too much!* You might even want to put them in the refrigerator for a few minutes before the magic show. Put the pennies on a plate and ask someone from the audience to choose one, while your back is turned. Tell them to hold the penny tightly to let their "vibrations" flow into the penny. Then tell them to look at the date on the penny, so they'll know which one they chose. After about 20 seconds, have the person pass it to someone else in the audience and go through the patter again—asking the second person to let their "vibrations" flow into the penny and to concentrate on the date. Now have the second person put the penny back on the plate and then tell you to turn around. Quickly you will identify the correct penny!

How It's Done:

You will quickly pick up or touch each penny until you find the one that is warmer than the others. Copper is a good conductor of heat—and all those "vibrations" are really just body heat, transferred from the person to the penny!

THE LIVING RAISINS

This is a quick but dumb trick, so don't spend too much time on it. Just try to make your patter cute.

Tell your audience that you have trained six raisins to think of themselves as fish. They are now, believe it or not, The Living Raisins. And you can prove it by returning them to their natural habitat: water. They love the water, you say, but like all fish they must have oxygen to breathe. And since they don't have gills, they will have to come to the surface for air. Also, you might add that The Living Raisins are from California, and consequently they prefer mineral water or seltzer rather than plain water.

Pour a glass of fresh club soda and drop six ordinary raisins into it. Then simply watch the action! The raisins will rise to the surface and then sink again repeatedly. Announce grandly, "The Living Raisins, ladies and gentlemen!" And then move on to another trick!

QUICKIE TRICKY

Choose a volunteer from the audience and have the person come forward. Tell the volunteer that you're going to do a mind-reading trick. Then turn around so that your back is to the person and close your eyes. Tell the person to put one hand on his or her head, and then to concentrate on whichever hand it is. Use a lot of patter for this trick—because you need about 30 or 45 seconds for the trick to work. Keep saying, "Are you concentrating on the hand?" Finally, tell the volunteer to put

his or her hand down. Then turn around and quickly ask to see both hands—palms up. Miraculously, you will announce which hand was on the person's head!

How It's Done:
The palm that is lighter in color will be the one that was on the person's head. Why? Because blood didn't circulate as much in the hand that was up in the air.

DRAGON BREATH
Tell the audience that you have Dragon Breath, which allows you to heat things up simply by blowing on them. In fact, you say, you can make water boil in a glass just by touching it with your finger— once your finger has been heated up with Dragon Breath, of course.

To perform the trick, have a small glass of water and a *wet* handkerchief ready. The glass of water should be about two-thirds full. Cover the glass with the handkerchief and push it down into the glass until the cloth touches the surface of the water. Then hold the glass as shown, with one hand flat over the mouth of the glass and the other hand tightly wrapped around the handkerchief and glass, near the rim. Turn the glass over quickly. A little water might

PICK A PENNY AND HOLD IT TIGHTLY AND...

LET THE VIBRATIONS FLOW INTO IT!

HAVE YOU EVER TRAINED A PET?

WELL... I HAVE TRAINED THESE RAISINS.

PUT-YOUR HAND ON YOUR HEAD AND CONCEN-TRATE ON YOUR HAND!

I HAVE MY BACK TO YOU AND I AM NOT LOOKING.

RAISINS

GOLDEN SUN

ST/88

HANKERCHIEF AROUND GLASS | TURN GLASS UPSIDE-DOWN | INDEX FINGER

come out, but most of it will stay in the glass.

Now take away one hand—the one that was flat over the opening. Hold the glass and handkerchief near the rim—still upside down—and breathe your Dragon Breath on the index finger of your free hand. Then push down on the top of the glass (it's really the bottom, but it's upside down). Say, "Boil, boil, boil and bubble." The water should start bubbling, but if it doesn't, breathe on your finger again and push harder. Hold tight. The glass must slip down a little but the handkerchief must not move for the "boiling" effect to happen.

MAGICIAN'S NO. 1, MOST IMPORTANT RULE IN THE WHOLE WORLD

Never repeat a trick!

AFTERWORDS

Here are the secrets to the other amazing tricks in your Science Magic Show. It's up to you whether or not you want to reveal to your audience just how these spectacular tricks work.

The Living Raisins

The club soda you used for this trick contains a lot of bubbles, which are really the gas *carbon dioxide*. Bubbles tend to collect on the surfaces of things. So when you dropped raisins into the glass, the bubbles collected on the raisins and lifted them to the top of the liquid. But at the top, the bubbles break and the carbon dioxide is released into the air, so the raisins sink back down again.

Why do the bubbles lift the raisins up? Because when they attach themselves to the raisin, they increase the raisin's volume without increasing its weight very much. Now that the raisin-plus-bubbles is bigger, it displaces more water. Things that displace enough water to equal their own weight will float. So the "bigger" raisin will float. When the bubbles that were clinging to the raisin burst at the surface, the raisin becomes smaller. Now it doesn't displace enough water to equal its own weight, so it sinks. This trick can also be done with salted peanuts and any carbonated soft drink.

Dragon Breath

Oooh…there are so many mysteries about this trick! Why doesn't the water fall out of the glass when you turn it upside down? That's easy: It has to do with *surface tension*. Have you ever noticed that you can fill a glass of water *past* the rim and it won't overflow? Water molecules tend to want to stay together rather than separate. So when you carefully add more water to the glass, the surface bulges up but doesn't spill over because the molecules would rather stick together than spread out all over the place. That's surface tension. In the Dragon Breath trick, you've got surface tension—even with the glass upside down. The water fills in each tiny space between the handkerchief, and creates hundreds of little areas with enough surface tension to keep the water in the glass.

But what makes the water seem to boil? Air pressure, coming from outside the glass, is pushing up on the handkerchief and the water. When you push down on the glass, you cause the water level to drop and you create a space where there isn't any water. So air flows in through the handkerchief to equalize the pressure inside the glass. As the air moves up through the water to reach the "empty" space at the top of the glass, it looks like the water is boiling. And *you* look like a magician!

COLOR & LIGHT

COLOR & LIGHT

Roses are red,
Violets are blue,
We have a Color
Activity for you!
You'll need about 45 minutes
to make and experiment
with color wheels.

YOU WILL NEED

3 Flashlights (borrow from
    friends)
Balloons in four colors: red,
    yellow, green, and blue
Scissors
Heavy white paper
Compass for drawing circles
Ruler and pencil
Crayons or felt-tip markers
    in all colors
Hand-cranked drill and
    drill bit

Note: If you don't have a
hand drill, you can spin your
color wheels with a piece of
string as shown on page 86.

What color is white? Most
people think that white is
no color. But the truth is that
white is the color you see
when *all* the colors of the
rainbow are reflected at
once. You can trick your eyes

(and brain) into seeing white
by looking at all of the rainbow colors at the exact
same time. If the colors are
spinning around so fast that
you can't really see them
separately, your brain will put
them together and see white.
Try it and *see!*

1 Is white light really
white? Or is it made
up of many different
colors? To find out, try mixing colored lights and see
what you get. With the scissors, cut the necks off of
some colored balloons.
Stretch a red balloon across
one flashlight so that it makes
red light. Stretch a yellow or
green balloon across another
flashlight, and a blue balloon
across the third flashlight.
Turn out the room lights and
shine the red light at a white
wall or white piece of paper.
Do you see a red spot? Now
shine the blue flashlight at
the same spot, so that it
overlaps the red. What color

do you see? Add a third
color—either yellow or
green—from a third flash-
light. Which three colors
mixed together make the
spot appear to be white?

2 Make a color wheel
with all the colors of
the rainbow. Use a
compass to draw a circle
about 3½" in diameter on
heavy white paper. With a
ruler and a pencil, divide the
circle into eight equal pie-
shaped sections. Color each
section a different color,
starting with red and then
adding orange, yellow, green,
blue, indigo, and violet.
Leave the last section white.
Cut out your colored circle.
Carefully poke the end of the
drill bit through the center of
the color wheel. Don't make

a big hole in the paper, or it
won't spin on the drill. Stand
in front of a mirror, with the
color wheel facing it, and
turn the crank handle of the
drill as fast as you can. Do
you see all the colors separately—or does your brain
combine them to make an-
other color? (If you don't see
a pure white, it's probably
because you've colored
one section darker than the
others.)

3 Do you think that the
colors on the wheel
are just spinning so
fast that *any* combination of
colors would look like
white? That's not the case,
and you can prove it to
yourself by making another
color wheel. But this time,
make one half of the wheel
red and the other half blue,
and spin it on the drill. What
do you see? Even though
this color wheel is spinning
just as fast as the other one,
your brain can see the two
separate colors flashing by.

4 Make a color wheel that *will* allow your brain to combine the two colors. Divide the wheel into eight sections. Color every other section red. Color the alternate pie shapes blue. When you spin this disk, what color do you see? Make another color wheel using alternating orange and blue sections...or red and green...or purple and yellow. Look at the Color Combos chart to the right. Can you figure out why these combinations will make you see white?

COLOR COMBOS

There are only three *primary* colors: red, yellow, and blue. You can combine the primary colors to make other colors, called *secondary* colors. But if you combine *all* the primary colors, using light beams, you will get white light.

Primary	Secondary
Red + Blue	= Purple
Red + Yellow	= Orange
Blue + Yellow	= Green

5 Make a Fetchner wheel like the one shown here. The easiest way to do it is to use a compass. Hold the point of the compass in the center of the circle the whole time.

THE FETCHNER WHEEL

Draw a curved segment, then close the compass a little bit (in other words, move the pencil closer to the point) and draw another curved segment. Continue drawing curves and then closing the compass a little until you have copied the Fetchner wheel. Make the lines dark using a black felt-tipped pen or crayon. Be sure that you can see the white spaces between the curved lines.

Spin the Fetchner wheel *at a moderate speed* using the hand-crank drill. Don't spin it too fast. Do you see some thin lines of color? Spin the wheel in the op-

GREEN RED YELLOW BLUE

1.
CUT OFF NECK AND STRETCH ON FLASHLIGHT

2.

ST88

posite direction and you will see different colors. This is an unexplained phenomena—scientists don't really understand why it works!

HOW TO SPIN A COLOR WHEEL WITH A STRING

Use a piece of string that's about 4 feet long. Poke two holes in the color wheel, one on each side of the center point. The two holes should be about ¾" apart. Thread the string through the holes, as shown, and tie the ends together. Hold one end in each hand. Put a twist in the string by spinning the color wheel around and around in a jump-rope motion, as shown. Then pull outward on both ends of the string quickly and tightly. The string will untwist, and that will make the color wheel spin. Watch it while it spins, to see what color it makes.

TWIRL WHEEL LIKE JUMP-ROPE
THEN PULL STRING

AFTERWORDS

If you've ever seen a rainbow or the colors reflected from light shining through a prism, you know that white light is made up of many colors called a spectrum. Early scientists had observed this also, but Sir Isaac Newton was the first one to understand that if these colors could be separated by a prism, they could also be recombined by a lens or prism to make white light again.

Later, scientists discovered that each color of light in the spectrum has a different temperature. By placing a thermometer in the space just below the red part of the spectrum—a space that looks dark to us because we can't see the light there—scientists were able to discover some invisible light called *infrared* light. They knew it was there because it gave off some heat! Similarly, the space above the violet area gave off heat too. So scientists knew there was invisible light *above* the violet—*ultraviolet* light.

If light is like a wave, the light "waves" from each color of light would be dif-

ferent lengths. Ultraviolet waves are much shorter than infrared. The shorter waves are sent out at a much higher frequency than the longer ones. Therefore, ultraviolet light has more energy than infrared. In fact, the ultraviolet rays from the sun have enough energy to give you a sunburn!

Infrared is a lower energy light wave, very similar to a radio wave. These waves are often used to make lasers. A laser is a beam of light in which the waves are all exactly the same length, and, more importantly, they are all *in phase*—moving along together, like people in a marching band marching in step. This is called *coherent* light. When a beam of coherent light is focused into a laser beam, the energy and light is concentrated in a way that regular light rays are not.

In the spectrum, red has the longest wave length and the lowest energy, and violet has the shortest and highest. As you go through the colors in the rainbow—red, orange, yellow, green, blue, indigo, violet—each subsequent color has more energy.

Did you know that an object's "color" is really the result of which color of light is *reflected*? Take a red apple, for instance. White light, containing all the colors, falls on the apple, but most of the colors are absorbed. Only the red part of the spectrum is reflected, so you see the apple as red. But the apple doesn't have any "red" in it.

But why does the sky look blue? In outer space, the sky looks almost black, because there is no atmosphere—no dust or gas—to reflect the light rays from the sun. But earth's atmosphere is composed of dust, gases, and drops of water, which are able to scatter and reflect *some* of the light from the sun. Because of the wave lengths of each color of light, it is the blue light that is scattered most easily. So we see the sky as blue. At sunset, however, we often see the sky as red, orange, or pink. That's partly because the dust in the atmosphere is denser near the earth. The dust scatters the blue, leaving the red and orange light waves, to give us a beautiful sunset.

CRYSTAL RADIO

CRYSTAL RADIO

Tune in to what's happening —on your own homemade crystal radio. No batteries required! The radio can be made in about an hour and a half. And it can be listened to *forever*—or at least until bedtime.

YOU WILL NEED

1 Empty plastic film canister (the kind a roll of 35mm film comes in)
Scissors
1 Piece of corrugated cardboard, 7" by 18"
Heavy-duty aluminum foil
Transparent tape
Masking tape
2 Sheets of 8½" by 11" paper
2 Spring-type clothespins, or 2 large, spring-action paper clips

From an electronics store, such as Radio Shack:
50 Feet of 22-gauge solid, insulated hook-up wire
1 Germanium diode
1 Phono input cable with plug (one end of the cable should already be stripped)

Note: You will also need access to a stereo amplifier and speakers, in order to hear the signal from your crystal radio.

What's a crystal radio? It's a radio made out of some wire, cardboard, aluminum foil, and very little else. The only mysterious thing in a crystal radio is the germanium crystal diode—and it's not really so mysterious. Germanium is a metal that can help detect radio waves. In fact, under the right circumstances, many different metals can detect radio waves. Have you ever heard of someone getting radio signals on the fillings in their teeth? Or on their braces? It can happen!

However, let's just stick to getting radio signals on a homemade radio. You could listen to your radio by hooking up a small earphone. But with an earphone, the signal would be *very* faint. Even in store-bought crystal-radio kits, you can hardly hear the radio sta-

tions you receive. That's why we suggest using your stereo amplifier to make the signal louder.

1 Start by making the coil for the radio. Use the point of a scissors to poke three holes in the empty film canister. One hole goes in the bottom. The second and third holes go on the side of the can, just ⅛" from the top and bottom, as shown in the drawing.

Now you want to wrap the 22-gauge hook-up wire around the film canister. But first, push the end of the wire through the side hole near the bottom of the film can, and then push it out the bottom hole. Pull out about 6" of wire and leave it dangling. Coil the rest of the wire *tightly* around the film can in

a single layer, until you have filled all the space up to the top hole. The wire must be tightly wrapped, with no spaces between the coils. There should be about 25 or 30 "turns" in your coil. Cut the wire, leaving about 1 foot extra. Push the end of the wire through the top hole and pull it tight. For now, leave the extra 1 foot of wire dangling.

2 Next you will make the radio's capacitor. Cut a 7" by 18" piece of corrugated cardboard from a carton. Try to cut the cardboard so that the ridges or corrugations are going *across* the short (7") side instead of up and down the 18" side. Measure up 8" from the long end, and draw a line. Use your scissors point to "score" (cut partway through) the cardboard along the line. Now you can easily fold the cardboard backward, along the line.

When the cardboard is folded, it will make a "pocket." You will want to line the pocket with a single piece of heavy-duty aluminum foil. The lining must also come outside the pocket and turn over onto the front of the pocket, as shown in the drawing. To do this, cut a piece of heavy-duty aluminum foil 6" wide and 17" long. Lay the cardboard flat and tape the foil to it with transparent tape, being sure to leave an inch or so hanging over the short end. Tape around all sides. Fold the foil over the short end and tape the edges down.

Fold the cardboard in half with the foil inside to form the pocket. The extra 1" of foil will show as a flap on the outside of the pocket. With masking tape, tape the

pocket closed along the edges, leaving the top of the pocket open. Try to tape the pocket together very tightly.

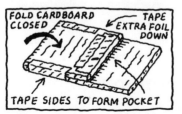

3 Next you will need to make a "tuner." Cut an 8" by 10" piece of heavy-duty aluminum foil and put it between two pieces of 8½" by 11" typing paper to make a sandwich. Fold all three in half like a book. The book will be 5½" by 8½".

4 Get ready to wire it all up! But first...you should practice stripping the insulation (the plastic coating) from the wire. For practice, use an extra piece of wire and your scissors. Cut very gently, until you have cut through the plastic *without* cutting the

copper wire. Slide the insulation off the end of the wire.

Use transparent tape to mount your coil on top of the cardboard pocket. Put it right next to the aluminum foil "flap."

Remember that you have two wires dangling out of the ends of the coil. One of them is 6" long. Strip off 4" of insulation from the end of this wire. Then tape it down *tightly* to the aluminum-foil flap.

The other dangling wire is about 12" long. Strip off 4" of insulation from the end of it. Now comes the hard part. You want to strip or bare a 1" section of this wire. With your scissors, gently cut through the insulation at a point about an inch or so from where it comes out of the film canister. But instead of pulling the plastic all the way off, just slide it down the wire about an inch. Let's call this the "bare spot."

Attach the *end* of the long dangling wire to the tuner "book" you made out of typing paper and foil. Slip the stripped end of the wire

into the book, near the crease, and tape it to the foil tightly.

5 Cut a new piece of 22-gauge hook-up wire to be your antenna. The antenna should be about 30 feet long, although 20 feet is probably enough. Strip one end of the wire and attach it to the "bare spot" by twisting it around and around tightly.

Look at the phono cable. One end has two kinds of bare wires sticking out of it. Find the one that is in the center and has its own plastic insulation.

Now look at the diode and find the end that has a painted band around it. (It will probably be a black band or ring.) Connect the banded end of the diode to the center wire of the phono cable, by twisting them together tightly.

Attach the other end of the diode to the "bare spot" where the antenna has al-

FIND DIFFERENT STATIONS BY SLIDING THE TUNER UP & DOWN

1010
1050
1130

CLAMP POCKET TIGHT WITH CLOTHESPIN

ready been attached.

There is another wire—probably a twisted one—coming out of the phono cable. Tape it down tightly to the aluminum flap on the outside of the pocket.

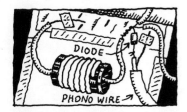

DIODE

PHONO WIRE →

6 Slide the tuner—your paper-and-foil book—into the pocket. You will tune in different stations by sliding the tuner in and out.

To plug your radio into your stereo amplifier, first turn off the power. Turn the volume all the way off.

Unplug your phono turntable from the amplifier. Plug the phono cable from your crystal radio into that input jack. Or you can simply plug your crystal radio into an auxiliary input, if your amp has one.

Turn on the power and set your amplifier to the PHONO or AUX setting. Turn up the volume until you hear a little noise. Slide the crystal radio's tuner in and out of the pocket to find various radio stations. When you identify a station, you can draw a line on the tuner paper, and write down the station's call letters or frequency.

If you have trouble receiving stations, try pressing on the pocket so that the aluminum foil lining pieces come more closely together. You may need to put clothespins on the pocket to hold it more tightly closed.

AFTERWORDS

It seems amazing that a radio can be made out of coiled wire, foil, and cardboard. But once you understand a few scientific principles, you'll see why it works.

Principle No. 1 centers around the relationship between a *coil* and a *capacitor*, which are the two main parts of your crystal radio. A coil made out of copper wire is capable of storing *magnetic energy*. The aluminum-foil pocket capacitor is capable of storing *electric energy*. When you connect a coil to a capacitor, the magnetic energy in the coil flows toward the capacitor, and the electric energy in the capacitor flows toward the coil. In other words, the energy *oscillates* back and forth between the two. The circuit formed by the two is called a *tank circuit,* because it acts like a

storage tank for energy.

But how does the energy—or the radio waves—get into the capacitor in the first place? That brings us to principle No. 2. Radio waves are electromagnetic. They don't travel on the air, like sound waves do; they travel on themselves by oscillating between electric energy and magnetic energy. Radio waves sent out by radio stations oscillate at the *frequency* (or speed) assigned to them by the Federal Communications Commission, a government agency.

When these radio waves hit your crystal radio's antenna, the electric part of the signal starts the electrons in the antenna moving back and forth. These electrons then produce a very tiny electric field at the end of the wire. You'll notice that the end of your radio's antenna is attached to the same wire that goes into the tuner (the book). So the signal from the radio station is being delivered through the antenna to the tuner, which in turn transfers that signal to the capacitor (the pocket). And where do the radio waves go from there? They're trapped! Now all you need to do is to change those radio waves into sound waves so you can hear them.

That's where the diode comes in. The diode allows energy to flow in one direction only. It sends the signal to your earphone or amplifier and speakers. Your speakers convert the signal to sound energy instead of electromagnetic energy and bingo! Out comes rock 'n' roll!

But how does your crystal radio tune in just *one* radio station? Why don't you hear them all at once? Because the frequency of oscillations between any coil and capacitor depends on the size of each part. If you make the capacitor smaller or bigger, it changes the frequency of the oscillations. You must make the frequency of your tank circuit match the frequency of the station you want to hear.

In fact, your radio's "tuner" is actually just a movable plate in the capacitor. When you slide the tuner out, you make the capacitor smaller. When you slide it in, you make the capacitor bigger. With a bigger capacitor, the frequency of the oscillations gets smaller, and vice versa. Look on your tuner: If you've written down each radio station's number on the paper, you'll see that the numbers get lower as you push the tuner in.

If your favorite radio station has a very low frequency— let's say 850 on the AM dial —then you'll need a larger capacitor to receive that signal. Why not make one? After all, it only takes a little more cardboard and foil!

NOTES

NOTES

NOTES

NOTES